THE RUINS OF SOLITUDE

Fig. 1. Detail from Hieronymus Bosch, *Ship of Fools* (1490–1500)

Published in 2024 by punctum books, Earth, Milky Way.
https://punctumbooks.com

ISBN-13: 978-1-68571-178-8 (print)
ISBN-13: 978-1-68571-179-5 (ePDF)

DOI: 10.53288/0473.1.00

LCCN: 2024946042
Library of Congress Cataloging Data is available from the Library of Congress

Editing: Eileen A. Fradenburg Joy and SAJ
Book design: Hatim Eujayl
Cover design: Vincent W.J. van Gerven Oei

spontaneous acts of scholarly combustion

HIC SVNT MONSTRA

LETTE
BRAGG

THE RUINS
OF SOLITUDE

MATERNITY AT THE
LIMITS OF ACADEMIC
DISCOURSE

p.

Contents

Acknowledgments

Writing *The Ruins of Solitude* introduced me to people who are ethical, open, and radically affirmative. For this, I am grateful whatever becomes of this book.

Jane Juffer, chair of my special committee at Cornell University, had faith in this book long before I did. She guided me through the crises that were part of my process. Grant Farred, to whom I first admitted the idea, "Derrida is a mother," helped me to imagine this book's existence, calling it into being before I knew its form. Saida Hodžić, whose generosity and care first drew me to her work, pushed me beyond what I thought was my most ambitious argument, pulled me back when I favored ambition over courage.

Small hospitalities make a world of difference to any writing project. On the days I had to bring my daughter to campus with me, Jane would bring games and puzzles to her office so that she could play while we talked. Timothy Campbell gave up his desk to my daughter when she came with me to a meeting to discuss a teach-in on Foucault's "courageous speech," minding her when she raised her finger to her lips when we spoke too loudly and she could not hear the show she was watching on my laptop. Trisica Munroe hired me to be the graduate assistant of Cornell's Feminist, Gender, and Sexuality Studies Program precisely because I told her how much my work depended on the support of the program. She recognized that to need support is not incompatible with competence or innovation. Thanks to all those who welcomed us when we disrupted your quiet spaces.

I am grateful for the support of many friends and colleagues, including Maria Aghazarian, Rose Casey, Adriana Camacho-Church, Steven Church, John Drabinski, Jane Glaubman, Jess Goldberg, Joe Harris, Matt Harris, Andy Hines, Stephanie Kerschbaum, David Kim, Jean-Paul Martinon, Jiwon Min, Colleen Mishra, Shailen Mishra, Svenja Müller, Nick Qaabar, Andy Ross, Margarita Saona, Jayasri Srinivasan, Jan Steyn, Amy Walczak, Sarah Wasserman, and Délice Williams. I am particularly grateful to Jessica Jones, best of friends and interlocutors, who carefully read many drafts of my introduction and preface, provided space and time for writing, and believed in the unblocked imagination.

My sisters, Christy and Shelley, made forms of touch and connection out of what we had available, sustaining me. My parents, Margie and Chris, fostered in me a belief in writing and language that has remained despite all my efforts to shake it lose.

I am overjoyed that this book found a home at punctum books, whose faith in the writing process allowed me to take gentler risks and to follow my argument where it wanted to go.

An earlier version of "Reaching for Being" appeared in journal article form. It was published as "'Beside Myself': Touch, Maternity and the Question of Embodiment," *Feminist Theory* 21, no. 2 (2020): 141–55. Reprinted by permission of SAGE Publications.

For you, my powerful child.
Your insistence on being yourself and tracing the world
as you live in it pulled this book into being.

Jellyfish Philosophy

A few years ago, when I hadn't yet figured out how to write this book, I opened my freezer one day to find an invitation from my daughter: *You are invited to a jellyfish party. It starts whenever.* Worried I had missed the party — who knows how long the invitation had been in the freezer? — I hurried to her room to press her for more detail. She didn't blink at my sudden appearance in the doorway. *It is whenever.*

Perhaps by "jellyfish party" she meant a *bloom?* Every now and then, jellyfish come together, and the sea feels clogged, and the space between things seems pink. We call this a jellyfish *bloom.* Perhaps this is where she was inviting me, to where the space between things is uncertain and bodies are indeterminable, one washing over the other? While I am used to being alone, for her the distance and space between bodies is a weight she can hold and show to me. She hates to be alone, and she is drawn toward groupings and groups, to the out of place and the nonbelonging. In contrast to our loneliness, a *bloom* is a take-over of water and openness, bodies coming close, tentacles reaching down. We search the world, a bloom of bodies, for ways to go against our solitude.

A few years after the invitation appeared in the freezer, I found myself mentioning jellyfish in a job interview, explaining to a search committee why I had pasted an image of a jellyfish across the top of my revised syllabus just after the start of the pandemic. As I explained to the committee, the week before classes moved online my students had watched Fabrizio Terranova's documentary, *Donna Haraway: Storytelling for Earthly Survival,* and they had been surprised to see a jellyfish floating out of place behind Haraway as she sat at her desk.[1] By pasting an image of a jellyfish on my revised syllabus, I hoped to remind students of modes of continuity and connection that survive interruption. Tentacular thinking and tentacular connections help us survive disruption as much as the structure and order of a calendar.

I encounter another jellyfish while reading over an earlier draft of this book manuscript. In the draft, I am grappling with Jacques Derrida's theory of unconditional hospitality, trying to explain how "home" operates on an ontological level. I am trying to explain how the possible breakdown of "home" is also an opening to a question of being and of all we know about what it is possible to be. It is my most impossible argument, when I try to think outside of what I know. In my effort to do this, in my effort to reach for somewhere I do not yet know, to reach for a being coming beyond what I know, I merge "philosophy" with "jellyfish":

> *"Home" refers not only to that precarious possibility of a place to stay, but also to a sense of belonging in a body, identity, nation, or gender, as well as to that philosophy-jellyfish of being and knowledge that swims a bit around and through all these things.*

In this passage, *philosophy-jellyfish* is the way I let being and knowledge come together. The hyphenated body-knowledge reveals something about the impossible boundaries and containments we expect of ideas. It comes where writing is trying to form connections that cross the boundaries we have set up for

---

1   Fabrizio Terranova, dir., *Donna Haraway: Story Telling for Earthly Survival* (Icarus Films, 2016).

things or that challenge the way we have built things. The jel-lyfish comes there where writing is a threshold of being, a way of learning how to stay. With *philosophy-jellyfish,* I am trying to describe the beauty of what does not at first appear to belong and to explain what it means to abandon one's defenses for the love of another's non-belonging. I am trying to affirm the things that seem not to belong, trying to see how they fit, what they bring, what they tell us, trying to see how their non-belonging is not a reason to correct or remove them but a call to change the world.

Long before she wrote the invitation, my daughter used to take her crayons and draw round blobby faces with long lines coming down from them on the white porcelain of our bathtub. "Jellyfish!" I would immediately think, recognizing the shapes. But, no — when she was a baby, she tells me, I used to wet her head. I suddenly remember how I would cry when I held her, so moved was I by her presence, so tired. I was in graduate school at the time, completing a PhD in English Literature, trying to establish mastery over my work, wanting this security, trying to make sense of things. From out of this story of my tiredness, she escapes, bearing her own sense of things: skin with water flow-ing down and, from this skin, a remembering, represented on porcelain like history. On the bathtub walls she draws again and again her jellyfish-tears-tentacles, changing my story to hers, a whole other experience building out of mine. Our memories come like crayon on porcelain, undoing the proper like the touch of water on skin.

I guess what I am trying to say is that philosophy, and this book, is how I say yes to a jellyfish party. *Or is it how I say no?* Why shouldn't philosophy be a way to leave an invitation in the freezer, inviting each other to the shapes and promises that emerge outside of the linear passages of thought and progress? What is the use of a philosophy that cannot respond to the invi-tation, that must originate with the lonely author? Does this move us beyond ourselves? Don't we love those who emerge despite disciplining worlds, fighting for their emergence? *Give me awkward love any day over graceful mastery.* I would have a different philosophy, a way of writing-being that shows how the world stays with us, even when we fall back into ourselves. I would name and swim with a philosophy that develops in response to the invitation we find in the freezer.

The paper on which the invitation is composed might also be significant. It is written on a sheet torn from one of the yellow notebooks I leave scattered around our apartment. The disorder of my notebooks reflects the way I write. I compose in fragments, trying to hold onto the way the world sometimes shifts out of reach of my representation and something beautiful emerges. The world comes always out of place, never while I am in my office sitting at my desk alone. Sometimes my daughter comes across one of these notebooks, and she flips to a page in the middle to add to my notes. Sometimes she responds to something I have written. Once, she removed all the pages and created a path across the living room floor to the patio outside. My writing becomes interspersed with her drawings and notes and stories and requests. My writing becomes a path outside. Who is writing this book, I ask myself? Who is authoring the philosophy I am trying to put together? What is being written here? Am I alone in the formation or the direction of this book? When I read my notes trying to decide what to keep, I often choose her interruptions over my composition. The page taken and left in the freezer becomes crucial, the writing that is not mine, that I might never have found, that I forget until years later. Should I cite it?[2]

Maybe it's clear by now: although everything that comes of this book came out of my relationship to my daughter, *The Ruins of Solitude* is not a theory of maternity. While it pushes back against the way we tend to dismiss motherhood as a source of theory — can't the mother be a critical theorist? — *The Ruins of Solitude* does not work to develop concepts from out of a maternal experience, even though these might decenter our theories of subject formation. Rather, by throwing into relief a dimen-

---

2   Jules Lee, "Invatashon," in *The Freezer* (2018).

sion of this relationship that is oriented towards what is strange and unfamiliar, the book considers how this care for what is strange requires an undoing of knowledge. In this way, *Ruins* interrupts the way we confine maternity to the familiar, and it offers another way to attend to this relationship. At the same time, it tries to bring forward how this experience is neither tethered to nor contained by maternity.

Ruins is about my skin and a turn of phrase and my tiredness and a book I read and the way my daughter mimics my smile and how she touches my face and how she bends her back when she stretches. By staying with these specific moments, *The Ruins of Solitude* works toward something abstract, the limits of knowledge production, and something alive, the nature of embodied subjectivity beyond individualism. With *Ruins,* I consider what it takes to confront the world as it is and how love entails undoing strategies of survival and legibility, even when this calls for courage beyond what I have to hand. We form across time. I inherit from her. I hold her up to my face, watch her walk away, sleep next to her — daily, everyday things that appear inconsequential, uneventful. From the specific comes a theory of resistant being, unfolding across what disciplines us.

The Ruins of Solitude is my ontological hope and epistemological experiment. *Can I be different?* Rather than trying to make sense of something — a theory of subject development or a theory of maternity — *Ruins* enacts the way I felt myself coming into being. I describe a surrender to what comes beyond my control and knowledge, and this allows me to use stories to explain my sense of things, developing a language that creates a window within the closed room of academic discourse. This allows me to keep my argument small and to lay it bare in its most vulnerable form, open to critique. What would it take, I wonder, to let be within my writing and teaching the way we are for others, the effect of others, the eventfulness of the event? What comes when we remove our defenses, full of fear and uncertainty, removing what would keep us as we know ourselves? What if we are allowed to imagine thinking in this way, liberation in this way?

This makes the book easier to read, I think, because none of us are now expected to make full sense of the argument. I do not need to cut you off from what you know. I do not need to ask you to negotiate your own sense of being in order to process my argument. The book thus offers relief. We don't have to be whole, now, all the time. We don't need a solid block of text. The boundaries between us can be porous. We can build otherwise. Something else will emerge. I don't need to know the whole world. My truth does not need to fit the whole world. I don't need to stretch what I know to the universe, to universalize. I can let be. I can fall, not a leap but a fall, detached from my knowingness, kind of in the world, now, exposed to its touch. *The party is whenever.*

To put my argument in its most vulnerable form, sometimes this is how we are, loving her who bends the rules that have been holding us up. *Ruins* bets its whole being on this claim. It imagines the possibility of being otherwise when, once, being could barely be touched. It imagines the outside of the apparatus when, at one time, the apparatus could not even be known. Weird, we could say — beauty as it emerges at the edge of normal. Through a phenomenological rendering of the arrival of another within my world, the book works to explore noncompliance with academic form and to affirm small moments that emerge across academic conversations but that get effaced in the generation of discourse. Through this phenomenological rendering of a love that cuts across an architecture of separation, this book works against the effects of critical thinking and of knowing. It works to understand the difference between love and knowledge. It works to leave academic form. It works to let me in, and her in, and you.

A Surrender

My ruin, perhaps, was inevitable. I read Jacques Derrida while nursing. When my daughter was very young, I used to read while she slept on me. She would wake in the middle of the night, and I would go to her and pick her up, and I would read while she slept against my chest. For the first few months of her life, I read according to the rhythms and patterns of her sleep. So it was that I read Derrida's *Of Hospitality* late one night, holding the book up to dim light, a small body across my heart, my arm curved around another's back:

> Let us say yes *to who or what turns up,* before any determination, before any anticipation, before any *identification,* whether or not it has to do with a foreigner, an immigrant, an invited guest, or an unexpected visitor, whether or not the new arrival is the citizen of another country, a human, animal, or divine creature, a living or dead thing, male or female.[1]

---

1   Quoted in Jacques Derrida and Anne Dufourmantelle, *Of Hospitality,* trans. Rachel Bowlby (Stanford: Stanford University Press, 2000), 77, emphasis in original.

Of Hospitality is a narrow book, and I could hold it open with just one hand, turning the pages with my fingers. My arm would grow tired, though, and I would need to put a cushion against the armrest for support. Or I would need to let it hang for brief periods while I rocked.

Has anyone tried yet to theorize the night care of an infant? Have they pushed back against *both* romanticized representations of care that forget constraints *and* quick dismissals of selflessness, finding a way to illuminate the effects of being at odds with a sleeping house to stay with a body not your own? At night, the semblance of routine and continuity of the day more easily dissolves. Any sense of control is tenuous, as sleep is clearly beyond command. Night care unravels. It is uncertainty, lost time, disorientation, fumbled speech, the breakdown of filters, the heady breakdown of inhibition and sense, reason's yield to another body.

Although we tend to think of the infant in terms of dependence and vulnerability, as an arrival we can hold and carry with us without deviating from our paths, my care for this creature effects the unexpected onto-epistemological disruption of Derrida's possibly radical hospitality. How do I affirm my daughter beyond her identification and determination, infant, girl, person, individual, human? How would I change were I to welcome her beyond what I thought she should be? What would lose its power over us? How does my tiredness help me let go of my expectations and my discipline?

Night care betrays not only the transformative and ethical potential of hospitality but also the radical effects of another's arrival on one's sense of self in the world. Reading Derrida while nursing, the body across my heart is an event. "'Come' is said to the other," and a series of knowable things that are bound up with recognition and the conditional welcome (the father, the law, the house, the host, the master, the proper) falls apart.[2]

---

2   Jacques Derrida and Bernard Stiegler, *Echographies of Television: Filmed Interviews,* trans. Jennifer Bajorek (Cambridge: Polity Press, 2002), 11.

Nocturnal reading and exhaustion and arrival and affirmation   *beautiful threats to paternal law and to one's mastery over one's home.*

* * *

This sounds beautiful but why is it ruin? And why are you telling us about it?

Let me see if I can tell this story another way. I was in the third year of my PhD program in English Literature when I read Derrida while nursing, and the experience compelled me to move away from literary studies and to write a dissertation that would theorize a poetics of arrival that reframes the maternal experience. The dissertation would be entitled, "Raising Derrida: Maternity Amongst the Ghosts and Strangers," and it would unloose maternity from an overly circumscriptive reproductive narrative, following the echo of theoretical thought through the intense intimacy of our relationship. While maternity is often thought of in terms of an embodied relationship firmly embedded in a specific cultural and social milieu, my dissertation would consider its affinities to feminist speculative philosophy, a tradition of thought that contemplates how the self exceeds the body's boundedness, coherence, and tangibility. Dwelling on the overlap of the theoretical and material that mediates my encounter with this other body, I would ask: what ethical and ontological considerations operate here beyond the bounds of my own capacity to think or make decisions?

When I tried to explain my decision, however, and to defend the academic viability of the project, I found myself at an unexpected limit. In place of a defense came this thing supine, the way we fall, sometimes, when straightness is no longer possible, a laying bare of some softness or gentleness that comes only in control's exhaustion. Working toward academic viability, all I could produce was poetry   *Forgive me, but she has been the wonderful ruin of me*

23

She has been the ruin of me   Signifying more than collapse, downfall, or devastation, *ruin* recalls the effect on the house of the unexpected arrival and can be understood in terms of a transformative poetics of arrival. In this regard, *ruin* evokes other figures deployed within critical theory and speculative philosophy to designate a form of liberation from disciplining apparatuses or dominant regimes of representation. Ruin is *undoing,* for example, or *de-subjectivization,* or *decomposition,* figures of transformation and resistance and liberation that take shape not in terms of accumulation or composition but in terms of the loss of some inhabited control or discipline.[3] If we consider transformation in terms of a capacity to resist or to refuse to work towards another world, to say no   *or yes*   then ruin ties this capacity to the arrival of another and to the forms of surrender and yielding and collapse that the arrival enables.

If *ruin* displaces my defense, it thus also enacts my argument. After all, a poetics of arrival argues that whatever we try to keep out has the potential to change the way we think and the way we are, arrival being a process that does not end but which puts pressure on a set of practices or ideas that seem natural or given. *Ruin* is an expression of onto-epistemological disruption that comes from the arrival of another and takes place in tension with composure and self-possession, modes of subjectivity that can overshadow the unexpected ways we come into being through fracture and gentleness, in terms of what is brought by the other. *Ruin* also emphasizes a particular dimension to transformation. At the limit, where there seems no direction, no possible cobbling together, nothing to hold oneself up   *"Come"*   transformation takes shape as exhaustion, fatigue, and loss, when one becomes too tired to stand up, when one reclines and inclines and falls apart.

---

3   See, for example, Stacy Alaimo, *Bodily Natures: Science, Environment, and the Material Self* (Bloomington: Indiana University Press, 2010), and Donna Haraway, *Staying with the Trouble: Making Kin in the Chthulucene* (Durham: Duke University Press, 2016). Ruin is close to what Mari Ruti describes as a "bad habit" of critical theory. See Mari Ruti, "The Bad Habits of Critical Theory," *The Comparatist* 40, no. 1 (2016): 5–27.

A *ruin* is just a thing not yet recognizable as such, a form of expression or being that takes shape out of place over slow time, caught between illegibility and uncertain survival, a mode of being whose recognition depends on different forms of seeing, knowing, and touching, a resistance to the real that allows us to say: right here, right here these two things *ruin and transformation* are the same, and our conversations and debates about healing and being-otherwise and resistance can now soften and change shape, and we will all be standing somewhere else.

* * *

I see how you re-define ruin, explaining it in terms of transformation. I am still not sure, though, why you are telling us about this. What was ruined, precisely?

I know I am proceeding so slowly, with stories and questions, building so slowly to my point, with such hesitation. I am not sure I can do otherwise. My ruin is not *mine,* precisely. If I try to own this ruin, to present it as a claimable, known object, presented here to you, I risk re-composing myself. I regain control. I take authorship.

There is also this muscular dimension to my argument that interferes with its progress. My arm hanging down from my chair, fatigued, is also part of the story, as is the way I search for *Of Hospitality* on my bookshelf years after I have read it, trying to remember if I owned the book or if I had borrowed it from the library, trying to find the passages I remembered reading *Do I even have the right text? Am I remembering correctly?* The bend and straighten of my arm is also a part of the story. My arm's bend and straighten is sign and consequence of my forgetting and uncertainty, both of which are erased if I present my explanation to you as this one, whole, coherent thing.

Perhaps it will help, though, if I return to the beginning, raising Derrida late that night.

When I first picked up Derrida's *Of Hospitality,* it was for educational ends. I was a graduate student preparing for a seminar. Reading Derrida while nursing, however, my motivation changed. Against a tendency to dismiss theoretical thought from the lived world, theory felt to me like this thing I needed to be living, like this thing I was embodying. Although I was originally handling this text in relation to my scholarship, I raised Derrida like a ghost. Like a child. Like a statue (*raze*).

When Derrida argues, for example, that the capacity to hear another is also a question of ontology, depending on a different time, I think of the way my daughter's stories leap across my understanding of some sequence of events. When she tells me when she is three that "there is a man outside the window," and I turn and look, and there is no one there, I must work to remember the person who came last week to fix the blinds of the apartment window so that the wasps from the nest outside would not cross into the living room. I must address the present from her time. Raising Derrida, I come to confront those times that I brush past her version of events, correcting her. I confront those times   *There is a man*   that my very way of speaking and ordering time   *outside our window*   renders hers illegible. In these moments, I wonder what I am stilling and effacing in my expectation that her sense of things and her way of being in the world conform to my expectations, which is also the limits of my frame of reference, or the way I sense time, or my inability to say yes or to imagine beyond what I know.

Reading Derrida while nursing brought me to the limit of my epistemological horizons, and I realized that what I know conditions what I let arrive. My experience of being confronted with the decision of whether or not to say yes is also an encounter with a subjectivity fused to forms of negation and self-knowledge, operating in terms of control and self-sufficiency. I was learning something about myself and about the relationship between a mode of subjectivity and the attempt to control others.

This is part of what I mean by *ruin*. It captures the way a construct of selfhood can just come undone, as defenses and armor and structures become suddenly dismantled, and one finds oneself directed away from the paths thought proper. While we tend to think about the potential of transformation, building other worlds, or being otherwise in terms of radical resistance or some force of will or of imagination   *or some beauty   some courage*   simply to say yes to her, or to have my palm against her skin, was to go against my future, against the way I cared for this future, the care I had already put in towards this future.

Forgive me

* * *

But what does ruin have to do with the dissertation? What can your ruin tell us about knowledge production?

Derrida argues that the task of the philosopher "is to try, by taking the analysis as far as possible, to make the event intelligible up until the moment we touch the *arrivant.*"[4] In this formulation of a thinking inextricable from ethics, the tangible body is the material limit of what we can make legible. Our reaching toward the other who arrives is both the drive and the end of thinking. In other words, the responsibility to make the event intelligible ends there at our fingertips, there at the emergence of another, there where something material and real comes to exist for us. At the end of analysis is the body touching and being touched, sense swimming up to surrender intelligence. This formulation of philosophy's end moves us to ask, *what emerges at the end of philosophy, where has it taken us, what happens now?*

In one sense, then, the event of the body across the heart could be considered the limit of my argument, moving me from philosophy to touch, from mind to body. If we take this to heart, then *ruin* is the moment philosophy (or, in this case, poetics) falls apart, where the divide is drawn between intelligibility and touch. That is, when I consider the limits of my capacity

---

4   Quoted in Derrida and Stiegler, *Echographies of Television,* 20–21.

to translate the event of her arrival into academic discourse, to find a way to explain or describe a poetics of arrival, I find there at that limit the body of my infant child, who not only cannot come into a scholarly argument but who also exceeds my desire or my capacity to make the event intelligible, being in her presence the moment of eventfulness that calls for more than its representation. Palm against the body of another, I find myself *ruined.*

If this is the case, I cannot write, legibility impossible, writing precluding the arrival of another, the arrival touching the limit of philosophy, of knowing. If this is the case, writing is the absence of poetics, its undoing, the absence of the other. As Derrida asks elsewhere, "can we love without writing?" As he argues, "to love the mother is to love without writing."[5]

Can we get off this path that Derrida sets for us? It's not good enough, right? Although establishing an ethical limit to philosophy that affirms the eventfulness of arrival, this path to understanding *ruin* keeps bodies and touch out of philosophy, dwelling on a divide between intelligibility and touch, between my written poetics and the *being-touched* of her body. Surely we can go elsewhere?

Here is what I argue: rather than only disjoining touch from the making-intelligible of the event, Derrida's assertion illuminates another condition of intelligibility, something that itself makes of the event and the *arrivant* these discrete concepts for our analysis. Rather than the limit of philosophy, the touch of another also reveals a condition of analysis and intelligence. Touch, to make this explicit, is also the moment we are no longer alone. Could it be, then, that our analysis ends the moment we touch the *arrivant* only because that is the moment we are no longer alone? Perhaps analysis and intelligibility end at touch also because they are themselves conditioned on solitude, fall-

---

5   Jacques Derrida, "The Night Watch (over 'the book of himself')," trans. Pascale-Anne Brault and Michael Naas, in *Derrida and Joyce: Texts and Contexts,* eds. Andrew J. Mitchell and Sam Slote (Albany: State University of New York Press, 2013), 102.

ing apart or transforming at the touch of another. The touch of the *arrivant* is the end of our solitude.

We can now imagine quiet complicities between intelligibility and solitude. We can wonder if the intelligibility of a subject depends on its solitude. Or we can imagine philosophy to be that enterprise which works within solitude, working always, if we are generous, towards solitude's erasure. We can wonder, too, whether the task of philosophy is conditioned on solitude, or if intelligibility itself might be a feature of solitude. We can wonder, too, when we are not alone, what replaces intelligibility? We can wonder whether, in prioritizing the project of intelligence over touch, we are not inadvertently keeping ourselves within a framework of solitude. We can wonder if, with touch, intelligibility opens up in new ways, so that we no longer depend so much on the philosopher reaching out his arm towards his object. What if *touch* and *intelligibility* and the task were themselves only legible within a time and space of possible solitude? What if intelligibility ends when we touch the *arrivant* because the task of making something intelligible emerges only in relation to a body we imagine being alone?

Love   *my refusal to explain the event, to make legible or intelligible the other body*   throws into relief a condition of intelligibility that is distinct from maternity or the maternal experience: a solitude of knowledge and body.

What we have, then, in *ruin,* is the decomposition of a framework of solitude that governs and determines the formation of knowledge and the possibility of making sense, of intelligibility and legibility. What *ruins* me is my incapacity to perform or inhabit an ontological solitude that acts as a framework for knowledge and discourse and embodiment such that what becomes legible is also that which can be imagined as whole, alone. Given the forms of thought emerging from experiences of skin-to-skin contact, from the efforts to think and write within the intense proximity of a bodily relation, I can no longer perform the ontological solitude that sense and legibility expect of me.

Ruin, in other words, is not only the limit of academic discourse or philosophy or the incompatibility of being and discipline. *Ruin* is also the emergence of sense and legibility beyond solitude. Ruin is not formlessness but the undoing of a condition of intelligibility we assume to be given and natural. *Ruin* exceeds intelligibility, or it illuminates the limitations of intelligibility.

To put this another way, rather than a falling apart   *a failure*   ruin is a critique of solitude, its apparent formlessness produced by the belief that we are whole, alone.   *Ruin*   is the visceral-ontological-theoretical rejection of solitude, a resistance that comes from the arrival and the touch of another, operating beyond and in tension with legibility, an argument against the form of its expression.

What would it be to bring into writing and argument and authorship the way the body exceeds its solitude, lingering touch of one on another, whole histories? What would it be to write beyond solitude? Might it throw into relief the possibility of an ethics that tries to reach beyond intelligibility, a philosophy that tries to begin with the touch of the other? What emerges or becomes otherwise legible beyond a solitudinous imagination of touch and philosophy?

When I write *ruins,* I write a subjectivity that emerges in tension and against the dictates of the academic form of the production of knowledge, the collapse to the self and the body as event, tied up and bound to the performance and production of writing. When I write *ruins,* I make a philosophical argumen   /   I make an ontological argument   /   I make a visceral argument   /   I make an argument that emerges beyond the time and space of solitude and its hold on legibility and intelligibility.

Do you see? Our expectations of viable scholarship are solitudinous. When we make a critique or write a book or publish an article or develop a theory, we perform and produce solitude. When I am unable to conform to the expectation of sense or of an intellectual or an author, I am also refusing an architecture of separation, and I need to express this in a form a creature might not viscerally reject.

* * *

I am not sure I know, anymore, the meaning of solitude. Isn't soli-tude only the absence of relation?

Solitudinous bodies
                              are bodies that we imagine to be whole when they are alone.

The psychoanalyst D.W. Winnicott argues that there is "no such thing as an infant."[6] He explains the phrase, less poetically, as meaning that an infant cannot exist in isolation. The original turn of phrase recalls Derrida, who took up the formulation in relation to various subjects   *there is no such thing as a real mother*   and it is an expression in which the avowal of absence in the face of purported presence challenges the episte-mologies that generate the term in question but that are unable to recognize its conditions.[7] Winnicott's declaration asserts that the attachments upon which the baby depends are constitu-tional. It is impossible for a baby to be a discrete object, without attachments. To say that there is no baby merely reminds us that the discrete body to which "baby" refers cannot exist without external support. "Baby," referring to the discrete body of the infant, has no referent. There is no "baby," whole and alone.

For sure, she leans against me, rolls against me, takes my face in her hands to laugh at. There is no doubt: me. I am patted and rolled against and slept against and weighed down. I am traced against my borders repeatedly from many angles and directions, emerging as this body within her sense, created thus within this field of touch and pressure, proximity and distance. A shape, a creature, constructed, but nevertheless there. A creature of cer-tain texture, moving with her from place to place with a rhythm

6   D.W. Winnicott, "Further Thoughts on Babies as Persons," in *The Child, the Family, and the Outside World* (London: Penguin Classics, 2021), 78.

7   Derrida, "The Night Watch," 100. Derrida says of the mother, "The mother was never only, never uniquely, never indubitably the one who gives birth—and whom one sees, with one's own eyes, give birth."

become hers. Without doubt, an identity, of some form. It is not that I am no longer human, exactly, although we test the limits of what this has come to mean. It is just that I am no longer whole, alone.

Here is another example to explain what I mean. Just as I finish typing this sentence, "This is illegible within the time and space of solitude," my cat steps across my keyboard and deletes the last few words of the sentence, leaving "This is illegible." A creature came between me and my work and the screen of my computer, between me and my sense. I re-type what he deletes so that I get my point across: "We are illegible within the time and space of solitude." *I move him aside; I am working.* I perform my solitude when I create my sense and legibility. My sense and legibility depend on the performance of my solitude. *I remove. I re-type.* My writing, the conditions of my sense and legibility, is itself bound up with my solitude. In order to become legible, I must first perform my solitude.

We can understand this better, too, if we consider the act of writing. Typically, when I write for an academic audience, I do so from a position that I build from my attempts to make sense for others of what I see and notice. This authorship is bound up with the processing and performance of this as knowledge, the product emerging as a performance of my discrete authority, my *authority-form,* let's call it. As I write what I know, I make an assertion of my knowingness. As I do so, I also inadvertently trace what my reader does not know, and I delicately keep this divide between us, correcting as I go the places when my singular construction could be construed as something else. As I do so, I also, maybe, delicately trace a divide between a reader and their world and their knowledge.

The form that authority takes to be legible erases the work and the labor and confusion that was part of its production. It erases my wandering mind, my doubts, the things I gave up, my shame, the lateness of my writing, my fatigue and uncertainty, the walk I took, rough bark against my hand, the weariness I feel at the discreteness I must perform, the weariness generated by the efforts to seal my argument, to create the smoothness of process that makes for clarity and form. It is not only that I am projecting a dangerous ideal   *this is the way I naturally am*   it is also that I am erasing parts of myself, erasing those moments of myself that take place for another, where I am the other to another, where my skin lingers as memory of touch for another   *over there, ghosts of my touch*   reforming myself into the legible wholeness and loneliness of my produced knowledge. I do not know why this is so hard to argue, but now I love also those parts of myself that I must efface in my effort to be legible to another.

To be clear, my concern is not only the exclusion or refusal of a body materially embodied when I write alone in my office   *here I am, writing this tired at my small desk, thinking of the tree outside my window, in a small window of time, thinking of other loves, other bodies*   but also the body as it extends beyond the time and space of its lonely material tangibility   *Here I am, drinking this water, with these memories of touch   sediment*

> *and*
> *with these*
> *absences, and,*
> *she*
> *remembers my*
> *touch,*
> *and*

where am I?

The *authority-form* I perform when I write as if I am solitudinous   *whole, alone*   prioritizes this body over others, carries forth this form of knowledge, bears these bodies, inherits and passes on separation as an expanse of empty space. The   *authority-form*   I must perform when I read cuts across the ruining world developing in each moment of touch, inheriting and passing on separation as an expanse of empty space.

The I writing   *this authorship or authority*   called up
by the defensible argument or knowledge production is a solitudinous form with a solitudinous body   *all these things tied
up together calling each other up*

It might be clear that solitude interacts with other examples
of embodiment that push back against Western epistemological horizons (such as that of boundedness, containment, integrity, coherence). Many times, for example, when we push back
against an imagined ideal of the human form, we do so by pushing back against ideas of the body's boundedness, integrity, or
containment, or against a subject's self-sufficiency, sovereignty,
or self-possession. We argue, *Let us see how we are animated by
the non-human of us. Let us remember how we are susceptible to
the other.* The ways we think of the human or of the body or of
the subject are circumscribed by lingering ideals of individualism or integrity, which foreclose alternative modes of being,
agency, and ethics. The concern is not only the way that knowledge production depends on a set of resources and conditions
only accessible to some. It is also that the modes by which we
know are themselves bound up with embodiment, how we be
and how we let be. We could see, for example, how Haraway's
cyborg could not write a dissertation, refusing beginning and
end, the linearity of intervention.[8] We could wonder, then, how
transcorporeal bodies survive logocentric discourse.[9]

While solitude echoes this disavowal of boundedness, it also
illuminates an additional dimension to this attempt to let our
bodies be more than the subjectivity we perform. In the search
to expand the legibility of embodied coherence beyond the
material body we imagine to be contained, my *ruin* at the body
of another throws into relief the limits of an imagination that
allows someone to forget how they touch another and how they
are touched and how this touch forms, also, the possibility of
that other, how someone is also the way one touches. This is

---

8   Donna Haraway, *Simians, Cyborgs, and Women: The Reinvention of Nature*
    (New York: Routledge, 1991).

9   Alaimo, *Bodily Natures.*

an imagination that sees the whole body as alone   *a solitu-dinous imagination, an imagined solitude*   that allows it to exist without tracing the afterlives of its contact with others.

Must we keep erasing those who come between us and our smooth sense, must we keep demanding their erasure to understand each other? What would it be to write in excess of this condition, without solitude? How do we write back within a discipline to a discipline without falling back into solitude? What if this disorganizing web of interconnectivity that differently brings things together   *this illegibility*   is another mode of response? What would it be to write from these moments of cluttering touches, from what frustrates our argument, from what leaves us supine? How could writing hold onto and allow bodies that come into touch in these ways, worlds that deepen by this touch?

I write the *ruin* of a subjectivity, undoing subjectivity, and though this is often seen as destruction and disembodiment, it is only the *ruin* of my solitude, this imagination of wholeness, alone, that holds up the possibility of   *I*   In the ruins of a writing, then, I trace the limits of solitude and what emerges beyond, refusing the conventions of a solitudinous enterprise   *coherence, intervention, defense*   all these things that tie back to me and my own legibility.

* * *

Just to make sure, though, this is not about how your maternity ended your academic career? There have been many studies documenting the struggles of families within academia, or the incompatibility of caring for a child and performing intellectual labor. Do you tell your story to throw into relief the challenge of being a parent and an academic?

Do I, in the end, make an argument about maternity? If I say that "I know the limits of solitude," I do not mean that *I alone* know these limits. I do not mean *because I am a mother, I know these limits,* or *mothers are those who know these limits.* What I

35

mean is: when I try to make my argument   *to make the event intelligible*   I encounter the solitude expected of bodies as a disciplining force, and I had never encountered it before now because I had never before known my own touch, or thought about the possibility of toes close to heart, fever as a patch of warmth against my chest, skin, reddened now. While this happened while I was a mother, it might not be limited to this. It does, however, make me think of my maternity in ways that diverge from the conventional. It does, however, make me think of my maternity in terms of my liberation and my revelation and my courage and my ability to think, create, and be. *Because I gave birth?* No, because a body emerged, and I cared about this body's being, and I felt my impact traced upon this body of another. *Does this only happen in maternity? Does it always?* No. *Can it happen in maternity?* Yes.[10]

Although maternity seems to build this fence around my argument   *containing it*   something nevertheless stretches beyond this fence, this fleeting thing escapes   *a cat*   What is tested is more than just *not-maternity* and what emerges with but also without maternity, without encompassing it all, neither defining it nor forswearing it, is also this shape shadowing across what we know, a silhouette of an argument. An authority-form is a figure of solitude, and solitude is only one measure of the intelligible world.

---

10 For discussions about maternity in relation to critical theory or liberatory thought, see, for example, Samira Kawash, "New Directions in Motherhood Studies," *Signs: Journal of Women in Culture and Society* 36, no. 4 (2011): 969–1003; Susan Fraiman, *Cool Men and the Second Sex* (New York: Columbia University Press, 2010); Lisa Baraitser, *Maternal Encounters: The Ethics of Encounter* (East Sussex: Routledge, 2009); Maggie Nelson, *The Argonauts* (Minnesota: Graywolf Press, 2015); Adriana Cavarero, *Inclinations: A Critique of Rectitude,* trans. Amanda Minervini and Adam Sitze (Stanford: Stanford University Press, 2016); Jennifer Nash, *Birthing Black Mothers* (Durham: Duke University Press, 2021); Julietta Singh, *The Breaks* (Minneapolis: Coffee House Press, 2021); and Alexis Pauline Gumbs et al., *Revolutionary Mothering: Love on the Front Lines* (Oakland: PM Press, 2016).

My child begins to feel so weighty because I realize that, just in the way that I hold her, I am trying to step out from a certain understanding of what it means to be human and whole. This is not an essentialist argument. I do not mean that my maternity generates this knowledge. What I mean is that she weighs on philosophy, too. The weight of a body undoes a form of knowledge as if the exclusiveness and world-reflectiveness of that form   *an authority-form or a declarative-form*   became impossible to uphold, intelligibility finally giving way to the presence of another, to the touch of the other. We could have been so many things. We are so many ghosts, such sedimentation of touch.

For example, I would say I haunt campus after her birth, but I do not even do that. My daughter is one year old and in daycare and I am walking down the corridor to teach after another night of two hours sleep. The coffee I hold in my awkwardly outstretched hand is at an odd angle. I cannot be certain that I am holding it upright. I run my hands one more time down my outfit, checking for underwear, bra, stains, zips. Someone steps in front me and I feel a moment of irritation; I am at my edge. I teach, and I walk to the nearest room to pump. I put my coffee mug in my pumping bag, gather the bag and my briefcase, and walk to my next class. What troubles me is that all that is seen of me is this single figure, solitary in their maneuvering across campus. My maternity haunts me but not campus. Meanwhile I, temporarily a part of someone else's time and space, am barely present. I am disjoined from this time. I am part of another's time. I am crossing times. I am out of time. As I walk across campus, though, I appear alone, whole, wholly alone.

Although emerging out of a maternal experience, the incommensurability manifested by my ruined attempt to defend myself   *I tried*   moves away from the ostensible divide between maternal and academic labor to critique a condition of knowledge production that is only coincidentally disclosed by the existence of the child with whom I found myself in relation.

In this way, the project is different from those that attend to maternal experiences to develop concepts that open up

philosophical and psychoanalytic explorations of subjectivity and being.[11] While these projects would no doubt help me
understand my experience and trace how a maternal relationship conflicts with knowledge production and the solitudinous
subject I theorize, I have a much smaller project. I explore how
undoing is also resistance and being. Although we can locate
the beginnings of *ruin* in my maternity, it exceeds containment
by this relationship, pushing back against the composure of the
authority-form to translate the unintelligibility of the moment
of touch into a bodily poetics of the supinely hospitable beyond
the rigors of the lonely present.

* * *

Is your departure   ruin   *phenomenology? That is, while
you are operating in the domain of knowledge, the effect of bodies in touch interferes in this phenomenological way, affirming
its own relevance to the intellectual endeavor of philosophy, and
refuting, as it does so, the invisible operation of legible solitude?
You are ruined because you can no longer perform the solitude of
the subject and so your critique of knowledge production emerges
as a decomposition of a bodily form, bodies beyond   I   in
the form of thought beyond   I?*

If I could re-name *ruin,* I suppose I would call it a creaturely
phenomenological experience, emphasizing its distinction from
a subjectivity whose legible formation derives from the tangible time of the body's materiality, affirming modes of formation
that emerge beyond sensed solitude.

---

11 For examples of these projects, see Bracha Ettinger, *The Matrixial Borderspace,* ed. Brian Massumi (Minneapolis: University of Minnesota Press,
2006); Lisa Baraitser, *Maternal Encounters: The Ethics of Interruption* (East
Sussex: Routledge, 2009); Irina Aristarkhova, *Hospitality of the Matrix:
Philosophy, Biomedicine, and Culture* (New York: Columbia University
Press, 2012); and Lisa Guenther, *The Gift of the Other: Levinas and the Politics of Reproduction* (Albany: State University of New York Press, 2006).

For Gayle Salamon, phenomenology is a method by which we find a way to go beyond our "schemas of knowledge" through the close description of sense. She uses this to explain the methodological commitments of phenomenology: "in viewing the world and describing it with all possible precision, we might see the world and all the objects and others within it open, and reveal themselves to be more varied and more mysterious than our imaginations could have conjured, or our schemas of knowledge contain."[12] As a methodology, phenomenology situates authority in this suspended place above and beyond experience, accepting a circumstance of the body in its very undoing of this circumstance, making of the moment of rupture the source of theory. It is a flawed methodology, always at the edge of its own dismissal, both hesitant and grandiose, both weak and extravagant.

When it resigns itself to the momentariness of the opening, however, it can be a guide. What it allows, as it slips through some small fracture it tries to pry open in a system of recognition, is a way of thinking of things or of making visible and tangible and sensible a way of things otherwise rendered non-existent by a smoothly operating *being-knowledge.* In this small way, it brings briefly into relief a condition or feature of this knowledge, giving momentary life to what is represented as unintelligible, unformed, incoherent, nonsense. It begins and ends at this body, not fully within a trajectory of scholarship that situates intervention in terms of discipline or field.

For me, moreover, sense exceeds my own body. While Maurice Merleau-Ponty reaches out his one hand to touch the other, reflecting on this act of self-touch, I consider the event of *being-touched* by another.[13] In this way, my ruin is not an account of my own experience, although this is close to what has come to be called auto-theory.[14] Critiquing solitude, I follow a creaturely

---

12   Gayle Salamon, "What's Critical about Critical Phenomenology?" *Puncta: Journal of Critical Phenomenology* 1, no. 1 (2018): 16.

13   Maurice Merleau-Ponty, *Phenomenology of Perception,* trans. Colin Smith (London: Routledge, 1962), 106

14   See, for example, Nelson, *The Argonauts.*

phenomenological experience as it emerges in tension with the ontological solitude of an authority-form that seems to align with the solitudinous discreteness of an embodied subjectivity.

In this way, I try to show that a sense of coming apart or of fragmentation or undoing, which appear to suggest the impossibility of a subject that coheres, are also the sign only of solitude's coming undone. It is only coming undone within the framework of solitude. A phenomenology without authority-form is a mode of expression within a solitudinous world that could otherwise never find legibility. The things we watch as we fall apart are also the signs of our creatureliness, of how the form for which we strive is also alone.

* * *

Why not just leave academia, though? Why give this account of yourself, which is an account of no longer being yourself, in the first place? Why write anything at all?

I could have simply left, I suppose. An exit is rarely smooth. It stalls and stutters, slow and awkward, over years in limbo, not knowing there is such a thing as letting go, of not holding on. Although rarely clean, an exit nevertheless demarcates and re-inscribes a limit or a boundary, a divide between belonging and non-belonging. A ruin, I think, refuses this boundary, or undoes this boundary. A ruin is a way of leaving that creates rather than leaves space. *Ruin* traces the fragility of walls, such that we can imagine better what survives these, rather than dwelling on their stability and exclusivity.

I do not depart from the academy, precisely, but from solitude. I am leaving solitude. It appears to be a departure from the academy only because the two are so closely entwined. What is the relationship between self and knowledge production? Why are these two entwined such that there is no way to disentangle them or make this boundary legible? What is the relationship between love and leaving? The book is caught between these two poles and the way they build each other up   *maybe I have them confused*   bringing each other into being, which opens up worlds in ways that diverge from all I have been taught and all the ways I have been formed.

Between love and leaving is an emancipatory poetics that comes from the unanticipated and the uncontrolled and also   *which is why I write about solitude*   from the ways we are encouraged to imagine we are whole, alone, with these architectures and apparatuses of separation, such that to touch another becomes revelatory.

In this way, writing-leaving-loving is a way to care against care. I write to actively care against any care for my future, the way I would hold it together. I care against care to keep me from my solitude, to keep us together, to push back against what would re-form us, what would create for me again the subjectivity of loneliness. The question becomes not what I can say or should say, but what I must say in order to survive beyond solitude: what doesn't fit, what broaches knowledge, what I can't say, what I dare not. To write as if one can be vulnerable is a re-creation, a remaking, courage beyond oneself. Writing with eloquence about what we love transforms what we do into an ethics that retraces our space in the world.

"Come"   is this something I am meant to stop saying?

CHAPTER 1

Writing to Stay in Touch

Every day, I clear my workspace. I gather up crayons, scattered paper, socks, and toys from under and around my desk, peeling off stickers from its surface. Each day brings this creep and flow of stuff into my workspace, and each day requires this reset. As I bend and stand, feeling for stuffed toys and small books from under my chair, re-posting my sticky notes, hunting for pens, I consider the role that boundaries play in my work, thinking that my work is, in fact, a study of the processes that dismantle boundaries. It feels strange to clear this space, knowing that the failure of boundaries and the unexpected effects of intrusion and the out of place are at the heart of what I do.

Clutter is more than disorder or haphazardness. All this "matter out of place," as Mary Douglas says of dirt   *all this stuff*   alters my relationship to the spaces over which I attempt to exercise my control.[1] The experience of things out of place disrupts my practices of compliance and integration. Clutter is linked to the possibility of the other, to the positive effect of not being able to maintain one's borders. Clutter feels, at times, like the relieving touch of the outside. A scrawl of marker across a typed sheet of paper is not a scribble or a

---

1   Mary Douglas, *Purity and Danger: An Analysis of the Concepts of Pollution and Taboo* (1966; repr. London: Routledge, 2000), 36.

mess, but the reminder (and the remainder) of what can strike a bold line across my thoughts. Her bright, bold lines across my work remind me of the precarity of my disciplined spaces, of how these spaces can become the material and backdrop for another's creative emergence. Clutter is a form of ghostliness, an overlap, one life spilling forth onto another. I let this other in, and her presence remains.

The clutter of my workspace is not only material. When I write late at night and hear my daughter calling for me, interrupting me in the middle of a thought or sentence, my writing changes. Even after I have returned from her bed to my desk, I am unable to keep out the inflection and claim of her voice. I remain in response to her, still responding to her cry. My writing comes out of and with the possibility of the cry of another. During the day, she climbs into my lap as I type, interrupting my writing with a pattern-less sequence of tapped-out letters *ggfhh[ygdjdj:sggsgs[[[[* These letters, brackets, and colons running together remind me of what can be let in and what can interrupt, demonstrating the pliability of my work. They trouble the coherence I presume my work to have. Taking Judith Butler in literal terms, they show a relation that "clutter[s] my speech."[2]

Does clutter have a time? Her time is like the post-it notes she sticks in rows across my office walls, an unexpected texturing and painting of moments within a duration, a deepening that allows moments to pattern in different formations. Hers is a post-it time that lets go of events so that they flutter and re-occur and demand shifts in thinking. This is a time of transition, reorganization, and shifting hue and depth. Events adhere for a moment within a narrative, but, as if placed on a surface, can be removed and replaced, so that I must leap, be moved around, be shifted from the past and to the present. Each moment hangs as if it might or might not remain   *There is a man*   might shift, might not address the next   *outside*

---

2   Judith Butler, *Precarious Life: The Powers of Mourning and Violence* (New York: Verso, 2004), 23.

our window   There is a cut and paste of time that suggests time itself might be a matter of surfaces, changing the texture and shape of the bodily present. Surfacing in the wrong places, a block of color refiguring first a white wall and then a green bookcase, always out of place, always marking a place, always a note, never inscribed directly on the surface but always amending it   *neither fluid nor static*   interrupting a narrative of development and of being, the formation of my coherence, my wholeness in the present moment, a trace of alternate stories, a memory.

Gilles Deleuze notes that children "never stop talking about what they are doing or trying to do: exploring milieus, by means of dynamic trajectories, and drawing up maps of them."[3] Decentering parents from the primary position given them by psychoanalysis, he situates them within this milieu as "simply playing the role of openers or closers of doors, guardians of the thresholds, connectors or disconnectors of zones."[4] Rather than me opening her doors, she is what happens to my walls. All around me now is a re-mapping, an othering of my enclosing surfaces, a memory of things coming together across time. Giant purple flowers on the bathroom door. Paper cups on the kitchen rug.

I would like to keep her clutter within my writing. I would like for her lines to cross this page, and for her letters to be interspersed with my own. If I had kept this clutter, this would be a different book. It might not be a book at all. It might be a dialogue, with a new reciprocity, an interruption that restages each time the terms of the conversation, the site of thinking. It would have been given to another, become shared, a process that shows the potential of our juxtapositions, our commonality, our communications, our differences, the unplanned. Her typed run of letters would be more than the reminder of what can be let in. I would incline towards these interruptions, welcome them in,

---

3   Gilles Deleuze, "What Children Say," in *Essays Clinical and Critical,* trans. Daniel W. Smith and Michael A. Greco (Minneapolis: University of Minnesota Press, 1997), 61.

4   Ibid., 62.

change them from interruptions to belongings, characters sign-aling the excited press of fingers against keys within a composed work, touch taking over from sense. We would follow these lines across words and off the page   *lines of flight*[5]

Even erased, though, the clutter remains. As Jean-Luc Nancy argues in *Corpus:*

> Bodies are in touch on this page, whether we want it or not, the page itself is the touching and toying [*atouchement*] (by my writing hand and your hands holding the book). Some-thing diverts and defers this touching infinitely—machines, conveyances, photocopies, eyes, and other hands have inter-fered—but what remains is the infinitesimally small, stub-born, and tenuous grain, the minute dust of contact, a con-tact that is interrupted and pursued in all parts.[6]

The dust of contact   It is not only that you and I are in contact, our bodies. I write also to come into contact with her   *dust*   while we are separated, there being no inter-ruptions. We   *me and you*   come into contact because of her interruption   *me raising the book*   and if bodies are in touch, it is because they are always out of time   *bodies are forming on this page*   It is the clutter that touches us, as if touch is a form of clutter, that which resists the smoothness of the argument, its coherence   *the ghost of her interference is what brings us into contact*   I write to keep in touch.

Against the solitude of writing
                              bodies are in touch on this page.

While we resist clutter at all costs because it gets in the way, sometimes a room of one's own prohibits thinking, the solitary

---

5   Gilles Deleuze and Félix Guattari, *A Thousand Plateaus: Capitalism and Schizophrenia,* trans. Brian Massumi (Minneapolis: University of Min-nesota Press, 1987).

6   Jean-Luc Nancy, *Corpus,* trans. Richard Rand (New York: Fordham Uni-versity Press, 2008), 46–47.

room without the clutter of the other and without the demands of the other leaving only the smooth limits of one's own thoughts and expectations and none of the deviations and textual imperfections that characterize the arrival of another. Writing sometimes takes place as cluttering, as the intrusion of things that will not be cleared away, as the sign of things that remain in spite of all this clearing away.

What world will arrive?

I lift her up, and we touch a ceiling, out of place, and I don't know what we touch in this moment or why, but I listen, I do what she asks, out of time and place and without sense, and, if I could, I would reach up to all the surfaces, away from our bodies alone, re-mapping worlds, just for a moment, according to the way we be.

CHAPTER 2

Reaching for Being

When my daughter was very small, I used to wake up with a start from a deep sleep and reach out a hand to check for her presence. If I encountered only bare sheets, I would be thrown into brief terror. The sheets were not a reminder that I had moved her (she was sleeping in her crib) but the cold horror of an absent certainty. I was certain to find at the end of my reach the sleeping body of my daughter. I knew she was there the way I knew that my own arm would be there should I reach out to touch it.

For Merleau-Ponty, the act of reaching out to touch another is closely associated with the possibility of coming into being. Reaching for another (an object or a person) demonstrates the possibility of what he calls "transposition," a shift in our sense of ourselves that occurs when we look at or reach for an object of desire. This shift makes us dependent on that object for our own restoration: "When I move my hand towards a thing, I know implicitly that my arm unbends. When I move my eyes, I take account of their movement, without being expressly conscious of the fact, and am therefore aware that the upheaval caused in my field of vision is only apparent."[1] As Salamon emphasizes,

---

1   Maurice Merleau-Ponty, *Phenomenology of Perception*, trans. Colin Smith (London: Routledge, 1962), 195.

while this creates a "decentering," it is stilled by the presence of the desired object, its persistence "as the focused and sustained object of my look."[2] A reach is "simultaneously disorienting, dizzying, decentering, and consolidating, purposeful, incorporative."[3] The end of one's reach for another restores oneself.

My reach across sheets complicates Merleau-Ponty's narrative of restoration and incorporation because the body that would still my shifting world is unexpectedly absent. As I reach away from myself, I settle not upon the body I know to be there, but upon its absence, which is itself signaled by the presence of another, alien object, the smooth, cool sheet. In this event, the world continues its shift and upheaval, the decentering has no focus or quieting. I am oriented toward and inclined toward a possible absence. My daughter's absence builds uncertainty into my reach, inclines me without end. My body feels out of time, its restoration delayed.

On the one hand, this is deeply unsettling. I yearn for coherence. A journal entry that I wrote during this time reflects this yearning, and it is filled with metaphors and descriptions of my skin. In the entry, I confess a desire "for smooth lines, for smoothness, no dirt, calmness, no bumps or ridges, nothing to irritate, to touch the skin." A few lines later in the entry, I restate my desire for "smooth lines." I would have "Nothing to bother, to shake up. Clean, smooth, fresh-smelling lines that soothe." The entry betrays an echoing confusion between my skin, the surfaces upon which I rest, the world as a surface I move against, the page on which I write, and time. The lines I discuss are those of the house, cluttered now, the lines of my body, and the lines of writing. Everything must be as I would have my skin be. Time, pages, and writing must all be smooth. Writing itself becomes a substitute for what appears to be a disruption to my sense of self articulated through the contours of my body. The focus on skin

---

2   Gayle Salamon, *Assuming a Body: Transgender and Rhetorics of Materiality* (New York: Columbia University Press, 2010), 53.

3   Ibid.

suggests a heightened sensitivity that veers close to the unbearable, a yearning for a lost ideal of my surfaces. To move through the rupture, to address the memories and space recalled by the continuous contact with a body different to my own, I produce and smooth external surfaces, created as such from time, writing, and thinking.

The entry recalls Butler's description of a subject that comes "undone" in the encounter with its ties to another. As Butler writes of the effects of grief and desire, the unexpected feeling of unknown binds coming undone, revealing themselves in their undoing, prohibits the possibility of self-narration, unsettling the I that would tell this story:

> I might try to tell a story here about what I am feeling, but it would have to be a story in which the very "I" who seeks to tell the story is stopped in the midst of the telling; the very "I" is called into question by its relation to the Other, a relation that does not necessarily reduce me to speechlessness, but does nevertheless clutter my speech with signs of its undoing. I tell a story about the relations I choose, only to expose, somewhere along the way, the way I am gripped and undone by these very relations. My narrative falters, as it must.

In my journal entry, faltering takes place through the act of touch and becomes manifested through the sense of the I coming undone. My speech becomes cluttered with images of the skin and with ideals of the skin uninterrupted. As I try and articulate my thoughts, they shift from my body centralized in my life to the surfaces close but removed that conform to and take the place of my skin. To move through the rupture, to address the memories and space recalled by the continuous contact with a body different to my own, I produce and smooth external surfaces, created as such from time, writing, and thinking.

The entry, however, betrays more than a flaying. When Renu Bora confronts the "liminality of space (and of materiality itself), on the borders of properties of touch and vision," he helps qualify my yearning for smoothness by highlighting its differing relation to two kinds of texture, "texture" with one x, and "texxture" with two.[4] In Eve Sedgwick's reading of Bora, "Texxture is the kind of texture that is dense with offered information about how, substantively, historically, materially, it came into being. A brick or a metalwork pot that still bears the scars and uneven sheen of its making would exemplify texxture in this sense."[5] Texture, on the other hand, "defiantly or even invisibly blocks or refuses such information; there is texture, usually glossy if not positively tacky, that insists instead on the polarity between substance and surface, texture that signifies the willed erasure of its history."[6]

My desire for "smoothness" is not only a yearning for containment, but also a lingering desire to refuse what is being given me: "information about how, substantively, historically, materially" I came into being (or of how I touch), a "willed erasure" of history. When I realize that I am not "smooth," when my yearning reveals this loss, I signal, also, that I am becoming situated in relation to my own uneven making, made to bear its scars. New texture for another, I am, too, newly texxtured. My accentuation of *smoothness* betrays not only an impossible desire, but also the abrasively restorative effects of being touched.

The last line of the journal entry, "Smooth sheets self of my skin," further transforms this narrative of faltering and idealized yearning from one of repair into one of emergence. Compact, sibilant, this final line   *Smooth sheets self of my skin*   suggests that all that is undone is the presumed smoothness of livable embodiment. Although the restoration is delayed and the sense of upheaval accentuated, the object for which I reach is replaced by something else, a surface smooth to the touch, without end, without form: the cold sheet. Rather than only a jolting

---

4   Renu Bora, "Outing Texture," in *Novel Gazing: Queer Readings in Fiction,* ed. Eve Kosofsky Sedgwick (Durham: Duke University Press, 1997), 96.

5   Eve Kosofsky Sedgwick, *Touching Feeling: Affect, Pedagogy, Performativity* (Durham: Duke University Press, 2003), 14.

6   Ibid., 14–15.

absence that denies proximity and asserts our separation, the sheet at the end of my reach for her re-traces my own boundaries, extending my sense of myself. In the stead of her body's reciprocal touch come other surfaces, the smoothness of bare sheets. A clear description of a strange sense of dispossession articulated in terms of skin, the line is, in the face of a faltering narrative, in the face of the lost linearity of the prose of the body, a metaphorical expression of confusion and indeterminacy that traces a newly sensed self onto the space of undoing.

Aligning surface, self, and other in a confused expression of presence, the line substitutes my skin with another surface. Rather than disavowing our connection, the mark of her absence, the ghostly indent without the body, the bend of the sheet, brings my body to another surface. Falling from narrative and giving up the grammar of the sentence, the line loses the subject only to change its expression. In the place of coherence, a poetics emerges   *smooth sheets self of my skin*   grammar the necessary loss that allows the articulation of an embodiment beyond solitude.

As Salamon points out, projects such as Merleau-Ponty's "must then be read as a radical unsettling of the Cartesian tradition that understands me to be a subject only to the extent that I am distinct and separate from others, where physical confirmation of that separateness can be found in the perfect boundedness of my body."[7] This unsettling allows other views of subjective loss and undoing. Confusion can produce differently imagined subjectivities. Dispossession can be the chiasmic experience of bodies that exceed material contours, that somehow touch at a distance. I resist the defensibility of a secure position in order to remember how I touch, remembering I had to learn to respond to ghosts to find her time.

One day, I stood beside my daughter, now a toddler unsteadily occupying self and body, and I watched her walk away from me along the narrow sidewalk next to our apartment. As I watched her, I stretched and yawned, my elbows out and

---

7   Salamon, *Assuming a Body*, 46

my head falling back from exhaustion. Soon, she turned back toward me, stopping on her way back to me to mimic my yawn. It is at this moment, as I arch my back, my elbows bent, and she copies my body's arc, that I feel in my stretch an alignment with her own stretching. I not only recognize, but I feel the similarity of our stretch, the way of our arc, and the stretch seems to belong more to her than to me. It is no longer mine, this stretch; it is an unclaimed stretching of a fatigued body, itself too much bent over, hunched as a matter of course, out of alignment, always leaning over.

My own body's response to its exhaustion sensed these movements to take form through her body, and it brought me into her space: a brief touch in arc, in pose, a kinship in pose that brought me again to her. The stretch was an echo and not simply a reaction to my tiredness; it was a copy, a reply to her stretch, her motion that interrupted and disturbed my relation to my own body. The only breach in this confusion were the elbows whose sharpness was only mine, jabbing, my own sharp bend to my own body. I was otherwise an extension of her action, a taking up and continuing of a stretch that began with her and that I recognized as hers. It unfolded over time, a kind of stretching time itself that imprinted the moment, that image of us turned toward each other, me stretching and finding myself once again in some extension or memory of her, through this very motion.

The relationship between these bodies is not one of mimicry or reciprocation. It is no longer clear whose sensations are whose. Expressions come with doubt. As I ask, at times, whose tiredness am I yawning? Whose stretch is this? Whose tension am I stretching? Can she stretch? Her skin is loose, without tension, without resistance. When I put my finger to my lips and gently pull, I recognize the gesture as hers, which I have inherited. The mimicry has inverted and I find myself as her repetition. My sense has become diverted to another, confused. I am no longer certain of my body. I feel her, a confusion of experience that relates bodies not along their distinction, but along their overlap, stepping over time and space in order to interchange experience.

While this seems to align with much of the tendency of thinking about the body such that its coherence is a fiction materiality dispels, or that material coherence is a fiction the skin dispels, it also suggests the way that one's sense of self can exceed a body's material contours, incorporating the surface of another. My skin gets in the way of the argument, decentering me and undoing me, but also restoring me across time and space, refusing the time and space of the tangible present. In place of coherence: poetics.

And this, in the end, marks the possibility of inhabiting bodies that stretch across time and space, only ambiguously possessed, occupying this bridging self. It shows that the smooth contours that enable embodiment are often ghosts, haunted memories of past containments or substitutes, impersonal lines of cloth, time, or writing that step in to determine one's sense in place of matter.

CHAPTER 3

Parting Intimacy

The first time I see my daughter, I am looking at a sonogram, grey lines and shadows forming the contours of her body. I am looking away from my body towards a machine and the representation of her isolated form. She is away from me and apart from me. The sonogram gives a new coherence to the body known to me until then in terms of her touch, points of pressure against some interior surface. As I look at her, a stethoscope pressing against my skin, I hear her heart beat, the sound of a shared replaceability. I hear her heart beyond her, identified and isolated as a sound beyond both of us, how we hear a part, how we hear ourselves apart.

For Rosi Braidotti, ultrasound allows us imagine the human body as "a mosaic of detachable pieces," an organism made up of disparate parts that can each be isolated and replaced.[1] In this way, ultrasound participates in a way of seeing the human that imagines it can survive its coming apart, working to "replace and dis-place the boundaries of space (inside/outside the mother's body) and of time (before/after birth)."[2] Carla Lam understands

---

1   Rosi Braidotti, *Nomadic Subjects: Embodiment and Sexual Difference in Contemporary Feminist Theory,* 2nd edn. (New York: Columbia University Press, 2011), 47.

2   Ibid., 49.

it similarly. For her, this visualization of my daughter away from me undoes "the boundaries of human corporeality that are the condition of possibility for one's relative autonomy and community," rendering invisible the "female body as organic whole."[3] When I stare at her image, I am split, losing my sense of my own boundedness. *We* are split, a dualism inserted between us that reinscribes Descartes's vision of subject and object: over there, the image of a body, away from me and distinct from me, creating a space between us wherein can enter the law, the unbearable outsideness of the control of others.

Facing the sonogram, I think of Derrida's argument that "We can replace everything, gestation, fertilization, the breast, food, milk, we can replace all the replaceable parts of maternity but *we will call mother the irreplaceable, as solicitude: there where there is solicitude as irreplaceable, there is a mother.*"[4] Describing maternity's replaceability, Derrida puts pressure on the longstanding idea of the mother's singularity. If the mother is replaceable, the argument goes, she is on the same level as the father. She, too, is a "fiction," subject to replacement and confusion. Although this argument challenges the apparent immediacy of the mother, it also conjures the image of a littered shop room floor, a relationship broken down into "all the replaceable parts." We are left feeling a threat to bodily integrity, a familiar suspicion of technology as it encroaches on nature.

Is there another way, somewhere between threat and wholeness? What becomes of my body and love if I follow my replaceable parts? Over the first few months of my daughter's life, I am replaced by bottles that carry, store, and supply my milk and by an awkward pump that I use in inconvenient spaces to express this milk. I am replaced by the cloth that wraps around her body and that recalls her containment and also my texture: soft. For a long while, I was always to hand for her. If she reached out,

---

3   Carla Lam, *New Reproductive Technologies and Disembodiment: Feminist and Material Resolutions* (Surrey: Ashgate, 2015), 27.

4   Jacques Derrida, "Hostipitalité," December 13, 1995, quoted in Judith Still, *Derrida and Hospitality: Theory and Practice* (Edinburgh: Edinburgh University Press, 2010), 131.

I was there. This immediacy, my always there of the world, is soon replaced by the mobile phone which helps me be imagined as always reachable, always able to be brought back into immediate presence. She says to me   *please answer when I call you*   Would I have known of my immediacy to another without the phone, which mimics and promises and so isolates and highlights? I had not thought before of my rhythm, my softness, or my immediacy to another   *my always there of the world*   as parts of myself, thrown into relief by their replaceability. My stomach is soft now, and my daughter pushes her feet into it   *I love your softness*   My replaceable parts decenter for me the necessary strength of my body, its hardness, my independence, my capacity for stillness, my distance. I am softness, transportability, surfaces, the awkward spaces of the world.

When my daughter was little, I used to hold her and rock her to sleep. She had an electric swing that moved with the regularity of a metronome, and I would try to mimic its motion   *Sway, abrupt stop, swing back the other way*   Standing in our darkening living room, I would rock from side to side for hours. My back would ache and my muscles strain, and I would be dimly aware of my dogs weaving around my legs and around the furniture, but her cries would continue, unchanged. After a while, I would begin to lose sense of time and my fatigue, and I would become myself caught up in the metronymic rhythm that I was emulating. Swaying, I respond, and this response overwhelms me, so that, for a period, all I am is swaying. I sway, and I am myself held up by this swaying.

It is not only that when I sway, I destabilize myself, or let give way my sense of myself, my control over my own muscles. A sway is not only a measure of time that repeats rather than progresses. When I sway, I am mimicking the chair designed to mimic me. That soft swing in the corner of the room suspended between two metal legs substitutes for me when I am tired. It allows me to take a break from myself, to sit for a while. I put her in it, and I sit facing her as she swings from side to side, watching her as she watches me, swinging from side to side. The chair replaces not only the arms that hold her but the body that contained her. There is something of my own, something bound up with my corporeal embodiment and the length of my stride, that is performed by its swing. Its nonhuman, engineered, Graco Slim Spaces™ "adjust the speed" rhythm is intended to recall for her not only my arms as I hold her and sway, but also my body as I walk, as that which carried her suspended for so long. It is supposed to recall for her the months-long rhythm of her gestation. The chair in the corner of the room is a repetition of my interiority and an echo of our entanglement.

My swaying reframes the question of repetition and eventfulness, between a body and the technologies that take up for it, between an embodied relation and the objects and instruments that trace and support it in the world. My attempted mediation of the world   *I will make space for another*   is itself brought into being by an engineered contraption. I am copying my replacement, and my swaying is also my way of stepping beyond some organic occupation of my body. The chair reminds me of the potential otherness of my interiority, this part of myself, my walk, its separation from me, something we can emulate and repeat. There is not only an inversion of the mimicry that determines replacement   *I mimic the chair*   I turn to the chair's mechanical regularity to inhabit the rhythm that my child will find soothing so that she can find a holding that will help her sleep, so that I can give her a holding that will help her sleep. When I sway, I am trying to find the swing's technical regularity, divorced from my individualism or specificity. I am trying to find a rhythm other than that of my own tired body within which I dwell so completely, fatigued.

My rocking is   *over there.* In this replacement and this inversion of repetition, a space opens between myself and my interiority. My interiority is   *over there.* The chair has created a space between my body and a swaying that is mine and now is no longer mine and which I must sometimes mimic. My organicity is   *over there.* The intimacy of my own is   *over there*   and this space between myself and my own brings strangeness to this intimacy, opens it. Over there, I sway, my swaying is   *over there.* Over there my hold, my holding is   *over there.*

In "The Intruder," Jean-Luc Nancy meditates on the effect of a heart transplant on the interiority his body seems to promise. Foregrounding the travel of his heart across the bounds of his body, he dwells on the strangeness of this organ once so closely his own. After the transplant, the heart remains like an intruder who "does not stop: he continues to come, and his coming does not stop intruding in some way: in other words, without right or familiarity, not according to custom, being, on the contrary, a disturbance, a trouble in the midst of intimacy."[5] For Nancy, his heart will always intrude, and the persistence of this intrusion will undo the time of the event. It will undo its eventfulness and arrival, as well as the time of healing and repair, the return to wholeness. The heart will not stop intruding.

Although we can understand intrusion in terms of a distressing interruption of a possessed sense of self, Nancy's meditation on an arrival that does not stop arriving also traces a temporality of strangeness. With the intruder, a heart that is both his and not-his, Nancy follows the time of intrusion against a more linear narrative of healing, contrasting the time of intrusion with the measured completeness of his functioning body. Against the time of arrival and the return to wholeness, Nancy describes, we could say, the time of strangeness   *his coming does not stop intruding*   It is a strange time, the time of strangeness, its own time. This time of strangeness shadows the moment of arrival, elongating past this event, out of one's control. This time precludes or belies arrival, for the stranger's "coming does not stop: he continues to come…."[6]

In a peculiar echo of Nancy, where I recall Nancy in this strange way, as if his heart does, indeed, not stop intruding, so my daughter's heart within me/without me intrudes and does

5   Jean-Luc Nancy, *Corpus,* trans. Richard Rand (New York: Fordham University Press, 2008), 161.

6   Ibid.

not stop intruding. Years after the ultrasound, when she has long been walking and ranging far beyond me, she brings her body close to mine and asks me to put my hand over her chest to feel her heart beat. When I do so, when I place my palm across her chest   *Can you feel it?*   there is an echo of the ultrasound, my hand reaching out to touch her, her heart beyond me. There is an uncanny passage, a sense of lingering on, of a ghostly surviving beyond myself. Her heart is still within and without me   *over there.*

While it appears to "replace and displace" us   *my maternity, my body in this reproductive process, her within me, connected in various ways, a weight*   this opening of a gap between what I imagined and sensed as close and interwoven illuminates a strangeness that at once survives and enables the close, the possibility of intimacy, of touch. I continue to feel the possible proximity of this heart that ranges far beyond my orbit. The heart beating beyond my body during the ultrasound is beyond me and within me, and this strange beyond me-within-me survives through time. The beat of her heart beyond me returns a prior intimacy, as if the spaces between us carry our intimacy, as if our intimacy is always   *over there*

Our intimacy has a strange time, the estrangement within our intimacy a body that stays through time, exteriority made interiority. This strangeness is the "trouble in the midst of intimacy" that entangles us even when we are apart, the ghostliness of the trouble in "us." It keeps intruding even after it has been welcomed and even after it has left me. Strangeness is, perhaps, the very time of survival, time's stretch from the linear and the whole.

Can I care for the trouble in "us," the strange relation of technology and body, self and other that interrupts our lives, its own trajectory, its passage through time and space? It creates a new space for the soft, the collapsing and the yielding, a new way of resistant world-making that is difficult to imagine within critical space, an atlas of the soft and close, an atlas of repetition, different constellations, different intensities, which extend beyond our familiarity to map the time of our strangeness. Rather than

holding onto myself   *though we need this to survive*   I
attend to and care for my replaceable parts   *I care against
care*   noting how they push me to a more revolutionary love
and world, noting how they relate me to another, for the other. I
care for our replaceable parts to keep our strangeness and to let
the world be that to which the other belongs.

Merleau-Ponty describes love as a transformative process
through which we come to recognize another's existence: "Let
us try to see how a thing or a being begins to exist for us through
desire or love."[7] For Merleau-Ponty, love is the event of seeing
another, and seeing another is a transformative event. While
the intersubjectivity of Merleau-Ponty's theory of embodiment
prioritizes binding and entanglement over a Cartesian divide,
it also allows a residual strangeness that remains through these
processes at the heart of entanglement. The event of the other's
existence hinges love not to the erasure of strangeness but to its
emergence. To put it another way, the existence of another is an
encounter with strangeness. And the resistance of this strangeness to the known of the encounter is another way of describing love. Strangeness marks the occasion of love's being beyond
one. Rather than that which threatens or must be overcome,
rather than that which is under threat and impossible in our
welcome, strangeness is the condition and material of this love.

Strangeness emerges within intimacy as the disjunction that
shifts love from a measure of recognition to the survival of difference and distance within the close. Strangeness bolsters love's
limits, returning through its failures. In the face of the failure
of the love we once thought was our final undoing, strangeness remains, beyond us, a persistence that keeps us from
full collapse into our own vision of things, itself keeping us in
love. Within accounts of love, the strange should not be lost,
the strange which precedes and lingers after love, which can
come without love, which exceeds even this way of love, which
changes our understanding, our possession of love. Strangeness

---

7   Maurice Merleau-Ponty, *Phenomenology of Perception,* trans. Colin Smith
     (London: Routledge, 1962), 178.

is, perhaps, the very time of love's survival. I come to depend on her strangeness for my love. Love that is my own and that enables my emergence happens   *over there*. My love depends, too, on my replaceable parts, the spaces of strangeness that are the trouble of "us." My love is   *over there*.

Maternity, if I were to try to describe it, so I could give this name its power to call up this love, is perhaps the way we learn to love strangers, the strangeness of those we know, how we keep the strange in keeping it beyond us, how we love the intimacy for the trouble, precisely for the trouble. Maternity, if I would use this name to call up this strangeness, brings not proof of belonging and the consolidation of inclusive community, brings not the question of singularity and the corporeal, but the love of intimacy for the trouble it brings, in love with this trouble which brings one to speak, despite oneself.

CHAPTER 4

Too tired to deconstruct, I, instead, collapse, and that is the argument

There is this word that Derrida, I think, invents *auto-par-thenogenesis of a writing* and it makes me so tired.[1] Slug-gish. He uses *auto-parthenogenesis* in his preface to Jacques Trilling's *James Joyce ou l'écriture matricide,* working to re-define what Trilling describes as "matricidal writing." For Trilling, writing is matricidal because self-invention is driven by a desire to kill the mother, who is the sign and proof of one's conditionality and vulnerability. In the preface, Derrida tries to make sense of this while refusing to accept the possibility of a "real mother."[2] He argues that, as there is no "real" mother, writing must be attempting to kill or to undo one's own birth. Writing is *auto-parthenogenesis* because with writing an author is trying to invent himself without the scars and cuts and inscriptions of his own birth. With writing, an author is try-

---

1   Jacques Derrida, "The Night Watch (over 'the book of himself')," trans. Pascale-Anne Brault and Michael Naas, in *Derrida and Joyce: Texts and Contexts,* eds. Andrew J. Mitchell and Sam Slote (Albany: State University of New York Press, 2013), 102.

2   Ibid., 99. Challenging the idea that the mother is immediately identifi-able to us at birth, Derrida argues that the mother is "a sort of speculative object susceptible to substitution."

ing to undo his own birth. He is trying to undo the ways we are susceptible, the softness of our stomachs and how feet come to dwell there, all our modes of yielding into being.

As a critique of writing *auto-parthenogenesis* is built to be unpacked. Forged from different languages and origin stories, tracing the opposition between birth and writing through the fields of philosophy, myth, religion, and psychoanalysis, referring to reproduction without fertilization *auto-parthenogenesis* is a run-on, a train of beginnings. Auto: a prefix signifying self-production. Genesis: from the realm of epic and self-creation. Parthenon: the virgin's home, and the temple of Athena, born fully formed from her father's forehead. It ties these all together. To understand *auto-parthenogenesis* one must first undo and then reconnect its intended meanings. One must connect disparate traditions. One must give evidence of one's knowledge.

Although Derrida condemns matricidal writing, the complexity he calls on to describe it dramatizes the productions and twists of the matricidal authorship he would critique. As a display of writing that undermines its own creative potential in the erasure of its conditions *auto-parthenogenesis* leaves in its wake an emptiness *a vacancy* that is always pushing back against the possibility of an origin that characterizes matricidal writing. Even as Derrida condemns writing that takes place as the emptiness of dreamed origin, he does so through the dramatization of its strategies and needs. Although Derrida uses the word to condemn the traditions to which it is linked, the complexity of its formation *it is a run-on, a train of beginnings* remains part of this tradition, and the critique becomes a display of matricidal writing, showcasing the energy of inventive reading and knowledge, the convolutions and complexity it performs as inspiration. The inventive energy of this word enacts what it would condemn, refusing to cross the limit to another kind of writing.

It makes me so tired.

But maybe my tiredness is the point? Maybe   *auto-par-thenogenesis*   is *supposed* to showcase what it leaves in its wake. Maybe the word is supposed to showcase the emptiness   *rather than the unpacking*   the emptiness, the lack of support   t*he emptiness of self-invention, of matridical writing, of self-invention*   maybe this is the weight of the word? Maybe it is built not for its meaning but for its effect, created to leave in its wake the tired body. Maybe Derrida is calling for a tired reading. Maybe the tension he introduces within writing calls for a reading that would not increase it, unpack it, or expand upon it, but undo it   *auto-part... no....*   Perhaps this built word requires an anti-reading, a reading against itself. Maybe this is the point of it. Maybe my tiredness is the point of it, maybe my exhaustion is its intellectual, philosophical, psychoanalytic argument. Maybe my generated exhaustion is *his* critique, an example of why we should condemn the sort of writing that builds in and demands its own convolutions and creativity and connections   *It makes me so tired*   Maybe the phrase is an intentional spectacle of writing that undermines its own creative potential in the erasure of its conditions. Maybe it performs its own reflexive critique, tiring me out to leave me so tired that all I can do is undo it   *auto-part*

In the postscript to "The Night Watch," Derrida confesses a desire to give up writing. He confesses a desire to *resign   (re-sign)*   from writing because "writing is *cruel*."[3] As he puts it, to resign from writing "would be a matter of beginning to love love without writing, without words, without murder."[4] He would retire from writing because he would "love the mother" because loving love is the antithesis to writing because   *auto-part...nogenesis*

Can I love without writing?

---

3   Derrida, "The Night Watch," 102.

4   Ibid.

In Derrida's desire to "resign" from writing, there is the suggestion that he, too, is tired. After all, to write love is to write against writing, which can only be a tired writing, the writing that takes place after the legibility has been attempted, strung together, made possible, a writing not only of invention but of belonging, of creating one's own belonging. Writing love takes place as what survives, as what is spent. This is the writing of retirement. Tiring writing, giving up, the writing that remains its own resignation, anti-writing.

I would like to write from my exhaustion, as if I have been spent, physically eroded. *Re-tire.* I want to write from myself as crumpled in, my body, my folds, various ways of collapses, crinkled, like a ball of tinfoil, but soft, like a starfish. When I am tired like this, I can feel the world trace itself in and along the surfaces created by this crinkling and yielding, I can feel it move between thin capillaries and across expanses. I can touch it more and stay with it more, when I am not striving to get beyond it.

Maybe the point of *a...part...is* is to wear me out so that all I can do is let go. To stand upright, to be upright, resisting all my inclinations, moving past all the ways I do not fit, takes so much of myself. As Adriana Cavarero argues, "Philosophy, in general, does not appreciate inclinations; it contests and combats it."[5] As she points out, "in the theater of modern philosophy, center stage is occupied by an I whose position is straight and vertical."[6] When I am tired, this uprightness is the first thing to go, and I become all collapsing toward what I would, feeling the pleasure of things, my yearning toward the still and slow things, my happiness with the soft and the curled. I become infinitely touchable.

I would like to write from *that* place, not from the cleared space, with each sentence an effort, saying only what it can, with no energy or time to correct or channel, no energy or time to straighten it out and put it in order. Just enough, getting it down,

5   Adriana Cavarero, *Inclinations: A Critique of Rectitude,* trans. Amanda Minervini and Adam Sitze (Stanford: Stanford University Press, 2016), 1.
6   Ibid., 6.

taking it slowly and laying it down carefully, the way I lay her down when I am especially tired, scared I might fall, scared I might get dizzy and bump her, scared, scared of my limits.

I lay writing down with all these tremors and shakes, finding in the collapse not the fall of the upright body, not the shame, but a kind of rounding and relaxing, as if all the energy is just straight lines, after all, as if all the energy is just hardness, after all, as if all the energy is just space, after all, and what is left is what I no longer have the energy to defy: the soft being in the world and the way I can wrap about a body and write. Maybe this is the point of   *auto-...genesis*

I would like a resigned writing, a tired writing that takes place after legibility has been attempted, strung together, made possible, forced into being, a writing not of invention, but of yielding   *I am not the strong one*   Tiring writing, giving up, the writing that remains its own resignation, a ruin of writing   *auto-partheno...a tired rocking*   This writing takes up for love when love gets tired, keeping and tracing the strangeness of the other that keeps me in ruins, keeps me from being whole and complete and alone   *still creatures.*

I would write when all my controlling energy has been drained away. Then I would be left only with what I would say. And what I would say is so small, so small and crinkly, so bare, so there   *Am I describing my brain, this organ whose shape suddenly takes over? Am I so exposed? Thinking has taken over and the exhaustion is gone*

Am I describing the womb?[7]

Without meaning, without significance, just the feel of the world amidst which I fold myself and fold into myself. Low, slow writing of continuation without means, of going without energy, of

---

7   See Ettinger, for example, who sees the womb in terms of "the human potentiality for differentiation-in-co-emergence. Its space is not a maternal 'container,' its time is not the inaccessible chronological past. It is the space and time of subjectivization in co-emergence." Bracha Ettinger, "Matrixial Trans-subjectivity," *Theory, Culture & Society* 23, nos. 2–3 (2006): 219.

having to be up when I would sleep, without imagination, without creativity, without thought.   *Who, "I"? This? Only this.*[8]

At long last

ruin

Collapse might not be a legible response to Derrida. It is not very articulate. It does not make an intervention. I cannot publish my collapse. Collapse, however, is another arrival, where we touch the other, an ontology.

What if we are writing against the lonely room in the house built for others, writing the arrival of a world   *re-sign*   a tired writing a tired body the tiredness the point the interpretation the way writing touches us the meaning and the significance? Writing like a starfish or like tin foil or like a heart close to the circumference, writing because *being,* writing because *tired.*

Against the solitude of writing   *...to ...art ...genesis of a writing   bodies are in touch on this page*[9]   a minute contact. Curling, yielding, letting in and letting be, writing to undo this dreadful solitude of form, of body. If bodies are in touch, it is because we are running out of the energy of straightness and boundaries and so we have also the excited press against keys of another's fingers within the composed work.

It looks like a body coming apart.

My thoughts slow, and I imagine that what emerges out of time and out of place and incomplete between great pauses has a way of living on, as if slowness and tiredness make arguments that linger past their articulation, so that they are ghosts that just slip by and return at the wrong moment. While I would be quick,

8   Jean-Luc Nancy, *Corpus,* trans. Richard Rand (New York: Fordham University Press, 2008), 162.

9   Ibid., 46.

I would care for slow ghosts, too, even as they get in our way,
trying to learn to remember, trying to remind myself, moving until I recall, living with my slow thoughts, my slow soul,
until   *clutter is a form of ghostliness*   *Auto-*

CHAPTER 5

Body-Theory

A journal entry composed in the house of theory, May 16th, 2021

Must I be a body in the world? Almost everyone seems to think so. They believe that if I can only get to the pleasure of my body and to the sensed experience of my body in the world, I will find a way to resist how I am taken up and created and conducted by disciplining apparatuses, and I will find for myself my groundedness and my anchor. My body, after all, is the place of my struggle and belonging, and I should seek to inhabit my body as it emerges in the world, beyond some idea deemed natural, beyond the law. I should seek to resist my alienation from this body. I should push back against any idea that too easily presumes we are all untouched by the world, that too easily forgets our mass and our yearning for touch and the chapped skin of our lips.

I mean, I get it. Far too often, we forget we are bodies in the world. We forget about our emotions and our sense and the history of touch that patterns our behaviors and our fatigue and our aging and the way our mouth still curls at the memory of a childhood fall from a bicycle. When your body is in the world, you can find a way to ground yourself in a sense of knowledge, to anchor yourself and to secure the possibility of thinking. A breath in   *lungs filling*   is sometimes all that you need to create the space and time to confront the negating harm of recognition, of the given world. To be a body in the world is also a process of resistance, a refusal of the ways we are asked or imagined to be embodied. Sometimes, we depend on our body, on its insistence on being present, on its irrefutable matter, its processes, its stubbornness   *I will be tired, you understand, and I will just lay you down here*

We count, sometimes, on our bodies, to keep us from forgetting ourselves.

But these letters come to me here almost daily, trying to reach me   *the body your material body*   asking me   *what do you touch? How do you touch?*   reminding me   *you are material you do not need to come undone   why come undone when you can stay together?*   They tell me that my body in the world is this thing I must hold onto, that it is a bridge for me, that it matters. It feels so precarious, this body, and I am told to care for it. I am told to practice self-care. They are long, complicated letters that take me hours to read, and I sit hunched over my desk, trying not to think of being with my love last night, trying to forget my desire, trying to focus. There is no divide between mind and body, I learn at my desk, trying to focus.

I mean, it makes sense to me. I get tired sometimes. The world comes to me through and against my body, and it shifts into shape in tension with my senses, as if we pull and touch each other. I recognize that I have this body, this corporeality, this age. While I would not be contained within a limited understanding of "body," I also understand that to feel at home in one's body is often the source of agency and belonging and subjectivity, the possibility of voice, courage, identity. I understand it is precarious, that to know one's own bounds and contours is never guaranteed, that boundedness is a thing for which we sometimes must work, that it is under threat.

Why am I in the house of theory? I imagine Butler speaking to me, sometimes, and they urge me to consider my ties to other bodies in the world.[1] They remind me of my vulnerability, and they have me notice the faces of the strangers looking in through the window. I imagine Merleau-Ponty asking me what I feel when I extend out an arm to a stranger passing by, touching them as they walk by. Do you feel like a subject, he might ask me, or an object?[2] Who is touching whom? he might ask. I think he wants me to understand that only when I touch others do I come to feel like some body. *I wonder how my touch feels to them.*

Didier Anzieu walks the hallways at night, full of goodwill, asking me about the scratches on my upper arm, and whether I know they exist because I do not believe my skin to be my own, whether I know it means I do not feel held together.[3] The red marks along my muscle have significance, I learn. They are a symptom. I feel self-conscious as I scratch myself in front of him, seeing the red marks across my arms and legs. From within the house, he is trying to remind me: you are lacking a sense of your own body in the world. You don't trust your form. He is trying to say: let me help you find your form, find security in your own skin. Let me help you feel comfortable in your skin. I can help you trust your skin.

I mean, I come to theory to feel my body in the world. This is what I don't understand when I read some of these long letters that tell me that theoretical thought is not the way to bodies or the real world. I read about coming undone and the loss of the subject and the death of the subject and it is all   *we need to be a subject*   I get it, but I read theory to learn how to breathe   *What if I love undoing more?*   Reading theory is also breathing, the letting expand of my lungs, the letting be sensitive and the flex of membranes and muscles, a filling up of

1   Judith Butler, *Precarious Life: The Powers of Mourning and Violence* (New York: Verso, 2004).

2   Maurice Merleau-Ponty, *The Visible and the Invisible (Followed by Working Notes)*, ed. Claude Lefort, trans. Alphonso Lingis (Chicago: Northwestern University Press, 1968).

3   Didier Anzieu, *The Skin Ego*, trans. Chris Turner (New Haven: Yale University Press, 1989).

75

my chest. Give me Merleau-Ponty talking about touch, even if I do so alone, even if I get him wrong, even if it keeps me from touch. There is not this simple divide.

When I fell pregnant, I wondered what everyone would think of me here in this house. After all, I am bringing a body into this world. Will they see the slow growth of my material body   *my mass*   as too much for theory to bear   *to carry?*   These days, when people see me through the window, I catch the surprise on their faces. *Surely,* I imagine them thinking, *your body makes itself clear to you. Surely, you don't have any truck, anymore, with coming undone.* Braidotti comes up to me. She is haunted, I think, by how we can come apart sometimes, without even realizing it, even as people care for us.[4] She is haunted by how we neglect the body's needs, its possible stretch into the world, the way it pushes us past the time and space we had allowed ourselves to dwell. This happens in maternity because people are not sure what to make of two bodies in the world, all entangled and confusing the beginning and end of body, of world, of being, of *in.* This happens in theory because we rub away the body's needs, sometimes, because we forget our own situatedness.

Winnicott pats my shoulder so kindly when I can't sleep or write, when my body in the world begins pushing me out past and beyond the space in which I had previously allowed myself to live.[5]

After my daughter's arrival, I watched the material changes ripple through the world. Beds lowered, mattresses moved from room to room, edges dulled, passages became blocked, others were discovered, counters became bare, locks increased, decorations became first scarce then abundant, glass became plastic. I watched the world reorganize itself into a space in which she could be, transforming itself to allow her infancy. I noted

4   Rosi Braidotti, *Nomadic Subjects: Embodiment and Sexual Difference in Contemporary Feminist Theory,* 2nd edn. (New York: Columbia University Press, 2011).

5   D.W. Winnicott, "Transitional Objects and Transitional Phenomena," in *Playing and Reality* (London: Routledge, 2005), 1–34.

how my sleeping patterns changed, my posture, my patience, my voice, my hair, my eyes, my tastes, the distribution of my weight, the rhythm of my walking, the strength of my thighs, my biceps. Without her, I knew, the barriers would fall, the muscles slacken, the walking would quicken and become regular.

These changes reveal the limits of "home," the false universality of the height of stairs. The stutters, shifts, and fractures of the home at the arrival of an another remind that the home is also that place that restricts arrival. The other in the home reminds of the alignments between ways of being and ways of doing, of the contingency of suitability and fit. The other in the home displays the narrowness of its presumed regulations, out of keeping for this other. The home is wrong, ill-built, unsuited for its inhabitants. The home is disproportionate, awkward, fragmented.

You know, I can imagine just on my own now her lungs expanding with air. I can let her body be in the world, as its own body. Being with her, I find this space and time beyond what I had cordoned off for myself, to which I had been restricted. Straight, trim, upright, muscular, quiet, proper, gathering back the oddness of my thought and movement, I now find myself the curving of the body's expansion beyond its given time, letting be all the breath, a relentless pushing of my body against what I knew of myself, some resistance to how I have been built to efface myself. From *her* comes the letting-be of breath, the letting-be of bodies in the world. After years of being hunched over my desk, reading those letters, all on my own, trying to focus, I finally get it, all of a sudden, my thinking nothing to do with it, everything the formation of her lungs and heart, secret beating heart: *body in the world.* Beyond what we are allowed to be, other than what we are conducted to be.

Is she a form of self-care, Michel Foucault asks. Is she your "counter-conduct," the way you go differently, the way you become otherwise?[6] By "counter-conduct," he means a way to

---

6   Michel Foucault, *Security, Territory, Population: Lectures at the Collège De France, 1977–1978,* ed. Michel Snellart, trans. Graham Burchell (New York: Picador/Palgrave Macmillan, 2009).

"struggle against the processes implemented for conducting others."[7] It is a way to care for those actions and ways of doing and being that go against what we are told will save the soul. Counter-conduct is one way we elude and evade, for a moment, the way we are regulated and conducted by disciplinary practices that have come to touch upon and blend with our desires, dreams, and practices. Counter-conduct is a change of plan, the incompletion of a plan, its failure. It is a breath, a turn away, a letting go of attachments and pulls, a slow intake of breath, unconcealment, but not in the form of my truth. *Is she your theory? Is she your body in the world?*

Rather than counter-conduct, she is my counter-care, I think, a care countering any care that has become caught up in a limited idea of what it means to survive. To encounter others, to be with others, I care *against* care. I develop a counter-care that would keep me oriented to what lies beyond, which is also what keeps me open to the other   *Her body in my world*   is a form of counter-care. More than that, it is a counter-worlding, the undoing of a world, its reformation. She worlds me, a theorization of self from other. Amidst the clutter of the house   *everything out of place*   we breathe these deep, long laughing breaths, watching the place undoing itself, as if it were nothing, feeling space and time find itself again.

To be beyond the space one had allocated for oneself, to love beyond the conditions one had set upon oneself, it is not embodiment in the sense with which we have come to frame it, the anchoring in self, in the matter of one's own flesh and blood, in the time of one's tangibility   *here I am, now*   My in-the-worldness   *this counter-care of another body in my world*   comes from the way she arrives beyond the limits within which I live.

Does this remove me from the House? Theory is another body, I think. It has a similar effect on me, allowing me to see the world otherwise. I learn how to build a world otherwise unloosed from my own body and to write my own survival of

---

7   Foucault, *Security, Territory, Population,* 201.

this world that moves me beyond my own containment, a world in which threat becomes the promise of vulnerability, some kind of wonder.

Theory affirms the world in a language not its own

At night, she lies with her arm curled around my neck to make her claims about the day. It is late, past when she should be asleep, I need to work, and I am worried about her being tired. It is only when I am finally able to turn toward her, to see her emergence there in her specificity   *short trousers, warm, soft pajamas, damp hair, open gaze, questioning, addressed, checking, asserting herself in that look*   that I can yield to her, let her be. In the morning, when I am trying to urge her past the threshold of the house so we can catch a bus   *I will miss class*   I yield, and I turn to her, letting the bus leave. I unwrap her snack and look at the acorn she has reached down to grab   *Why are we so quick to still our loves?*

I want to let be, to know that my love depends on my capacity to let go. I want there to be a daily and ongoing remembering of this angle and this space, of the beauty and presence of forgetting my own plan, which consists in turning to her, and doing what she wants, and going to her to see what she's about, in the middle of things and in the face of the proper. This is how I yield what I know.

My turn toward her is a way of doing things differently, and it brings about my resistance to habits and values I have taken up to such a degree that they became invisible to me. I do what she wants in the wrong moment and out of time, in broad daylight, and it is a strange act of exposure that interrupts the flow of my thoughts and my desire to conform.

I want to remember and care for the connections, angles, paths, interactions that accompany and mark her arrival, a period of settling, moments of presence, unexpected resistance, the ability to resist, the ability to imagine, the ability to hear an idea and to not immediately flatten it, the belief in the other, the limits of oneself, the transformation of failure into ways of being, the coming into speech. A qualification, a rhythm, an aging, an acknowledgment, a recognition of specific pleasure, disagreement, a turn of phrase, speech   these are the subjects of my care. *What do I know, anymore, of the precariousness of my knowledge?*

I want to care for my capacity to not settle into my sense of things. I want to care for ghosts and strangers, for times and stories that interrupt my own, to call these ghosts and strangers "relation as it survives self-solitude." I want to care for the out of place and for the interruption. I want to care for the disruption, for the laugh in the space supposed to be quiet, for the silence when we expect sound. I want to care for unintelligible images and spaces, for strange re-mappings. I want to care for narratives that do not make sense, for nonsense, for the forms of thought that emerge at the very edge of exhaustion, or at the very edge of love. *How much do I know now about the precariousness of my knowledge?* I can never know what intimacies are being forged, how things reverberate across time, how we are never reacting to just one thing. I want to care for all these things that get in the way of my progress and my professionalization and my form of life. It is a care against care, a counter-care, caring for that which makes possible the arrival of another world.

What is transformative and what is liberatory is just that which I cannot let go of in the name of my own legible future, something that has got a hold on me, this thing that holds me. *We are not the strong ones, the powerful, we do not always know, we yield, we slip, I try to belong.*

In the middle of a campus protest, she gets tired, and we head up into the building that houses my department, and we look down at the gathering crowd. She loves the crowd, the rhythm, and these different ways of coming together. Inside the building, she leads me down passages and upstairs, delighting in each closed door she can push through until we settle in an empty classroom, and we sit at the long table and stare out the large window at the protest below. She looks from the crowd to me: *We are alone.*

There are so many forms of solitude that I do not know what to say to this. She captures something crucial about our relationship, this sense I have of us hanging aloft out of nothing. I create verbs around her but there is too little material support. I give her stories on which to hang her thoughts and memories, creating pasts for these that outweigh our lives. I perform an independence that is beyond me, and it causes cracks and fractures elsewhere. Later, she tries to go to sleep on her own   *otherwise I won't be like you, able to do everything myself*   because she has seen me in the middle of things.

I am leaning into tiredness now and this is not nothing: to be with your body in exile from form is sometimes to be. My body is tilting now, compensating. Anxiety comes like another body for which I must care, as if I must always be with another body. Time, itself, is a body out of touch, lost. Solitude takes the place of another body, is itself another body, and I hold it, holding place, as we exist together. What do you do if the form by which you survive is harmful, what is the shame that you bear, how do you articulate this, what forms of expression become possible, how does this alter the words and voices of others, how does this open up the way we treat others?

Loneliness is less than solitude. Or, there is no such thing as a body alone.

Theory has come close to home, where I try just to write without defense about the simplest of things, bringing into expression just that which is, closer and closer to home, closer and closer to what I used to try to explain away, a palm against another body, finger pulling on a lip, a blemish, spirals we were once okay with making straight, the limitations and conditions of humanness. Theory, a way of grappling with a body's disjoin from a practice of worlding such that it will re-write another, is how I care against care. My turn to theory is a turn to world, practice in altered form, this way we try to care for the breach that enables survival otherwise, courage. I try to grapple with the past, being okay with fractures, with the draft, becoming okay even with the structure of pain that builds up in place of my skeleton   *another transplant*   this pain that calcifies and supports me through a new timelessness, because of the origin of another world that never stops intruding.

As a care against care, is this book successful? What might be the measure of its success? Rather than a subjectivity upon which I can depend through it all, I find myself at the end of ruins with a growing set of practices and orientations that stand in for me at my limits. Rather than the final conduct of myself away from a discipline come sets of practices and orientations that set up my love and courage in terms of a style of resistance to the ways I find myself conducted to know, even as I struggle to fully free myself from this conduct.

It is a turn towards her   *write your own book mom*   to turn always to the other and let myself go   *why don't you talk the way that you write?*   a thinking of the self   *she wrote this over ten years*   with a writing of the self   *my mom defended me from my shame*

Caring against care, I affirm the world in a language not its own. This is writing's promise and its limitation. It is its threshold, a space of emergence and of failure. I come here, to the threshold, staying with writing, not as the sign of the failure of language to change worlds, but as sign of one of the ways that resistance comes, too, beautifully subject to the invitation, undone, to develop a language of turning to the world.

I find myself turning to the things from which I am told I should defend myself. I turn to the way I seem to come apart. I turn to what interrupts my work. I turn toward what seems out of place, what should be managed and ordered. I turn to the material and to the small, to the moments of contact that we can so easily brush over. I turn to what seems to mark the limit of my belonging, and I let be what comes. I turn to what doesn't seem eventful, and I attend to its texture.

The world will continue to rush through the space now amongst my bones, where I am held rigid or unsupported, speaking despite myself, in hopes of myself, and in hopes of the other, keeping myself, like Nancy, "closed open."[1]

1   Jean-Luc Nancy, "L'Intrus," trans. Susan Hanson, *New Centennial Review* 2 no. 3 (2002): 10.

Bibliography

Alaimo, Stacy. *Bodily Natures: Science, Environment, and the Material Self.* Bloomington: Indiana University Press, 2010.

Anzieu, Didier. *The Skin Ego.* Translated by Chris Turner. New Haven: Yale University Press, 1989.

Aristarkhova, Irina. *Hospitality of the Matrix: Philosophy, Biomedicine, and Culture.* New York: Columbia University Press, 2012.

Baraitser, Lisa. *Maternal Encounters: The Ethics of Interruption.* London: Routledge, 2009.

Bora, Renu. "Outing Texture." In *Novel Gazing: Queer Readings in Fiction,* edited by Eve Kosofsky Sedgwick, 94–127. Durham: Duke University Press, 1997.

Bragg, Nicolette. "'Beside Myself': Touch, Maternity and the Question of Embodiment." *Feminist Theory* 21, no. 2 (2020): 141–55. DOI: 10.1177/1464700119853339.

Braidotti, Rosi. *Nomadic Subjects: Embodiment and Sexual Difference in Contemporary Feminist Theory.* 2nd edn. New York: Columbia University Press, 2011.

Butler, Judith. *Precarious Life: The Powers of Mourning and Violence.* New York: Verso, 2004.

Cavarero, Adriana. *Inclinations: A Critique of Rectitude.* Translated by Amanda Minervini and Adam Sitze. Stanford: Stanford University Press, 2016.

Deleuze, Gilles. "What Children Say." In *Essays Clinical and Critical,* translated by Daniel W. Smith and Michael A. Greco, 61–68. Minneapolis: University of Minnesota Press, 1997.

Deleuze, Gilles, and Félix Guattari. *A Thousand Plateaus: Capitalism and Schizophrenia.* Translated by Brian Massumi. Minneapolis: University of Minnesota Press, 1987.

Derrida, Jacques. "The Night Watch (over 'the book of himself')." Translated by Pascale-Anne Brault and Michael Naas. In *Derrida and Joyce: Texts and Contexts,* edited by Andrew J Mitchell and Sam Slote, 87–108. Albany: State University of New York Press, 2013.

Derrida, Jacques, and Anne Dufourmantelle. *Of Hospitality.* Translated by Rachel Bowlby. Stanford: Stanford University Press, 2000.

Derrida, Jacques, and Bernard Stiegler. *Echographies of Television: Filmed Interviews.* Translated by Jennifer Bajorek. Cambridge: Polity Press, 2002.

Douglas, Mary. *Purity and Danger: An Analysis of the Concepts of Pollution and Taboo.* 1966; repr. London: Routledge, 2000.

Ettinger, Bracha. "Matrixial Trans-subjectivity." *Theory, Culture & Society* 23, nos. 2–3 (2006): 218–22. DOI: 10.1177/026327640602300247.

———. *The Matrixial Borderspace.* Edited by Brian Massumi. Minneapolis: University of Minnesota Press, 2005.

Foucault, Michel. *Security, Territory, Population: Lectures at the Collège De France, 1977–1978.* Edited by Michel Snellart. Translated by Graham Burchell. New York: Picador, 2009.

Fraiman, Susan. *Cool Men and the Second Sex.* New York: Columbia University Press, 2010.

Guenther, Lisa. *The Gift of the Other: Levinas and the Politics of Reproduction.* Albany: State University of New York Press, 2006.

Gumbs, Alexis Pauline, China Martens, Mai'a Williams, and Loretta J. Ross. *Revolutionary Mothering: Love on the Front Lines.* Oakland: PM Press, 2016.

Haraway, Donna. *Simians, Cyborgs, and Women: The Reinvention of Nature.* New York: Routledge, 1991.

———. *Staying with the Trouble: Making Kin in the Chthulucene.* Durham: Duke University Press, 2016.

Kawash, Samira. "New Directions in Motherhood Studies." *Signs: Journal of Women in Culture and Society* 36, no. 4 (2011): 969–1003. DOI: 10.1086/658637.

Lam, Carla. *New Reproductive Technologies and Disembodiment: Feminist and Material Resolutions.* Surrey: Ashgate, 2015.

Lee, Jules. "Invatashon" (artwork). In *The Freezer.* 2018.

Merleau-Ponty, Maurice. *Phenomenology of Perception.* Translated by Colin Smith. London: Routledge, 1962.

———. *The Visible and the Invisible (Followed by Working Notes).* Edited by Claude Lefort. Translated by Alphonso Lingis. Chicago: Northwestern University Press, 1968.

Nancy, Jean-Luc. *Corpus.* Translated by Richard Rand. New York: Fordham University Press, 2008.

———. "L'Intrus." Translated by Susan Hanson. *New Centennial Review* 2, no. 3 (2002): 1–14. DOI: 10.1353/ncr.2002.0052.

Nash, Jennifer. *Birthing Black Mothers.* Durham: Duke University Press, 2021.

Nelson, Maggie. *The Argonauts.* Minnesota: Graywolf Press, 2015.

Ruti, Mari. "The Bad Habits of Critical Theory." *The Comparatist* 40, no. 1 (2016): 5–27. https://www.jstor.org/stable/26254752.

Salamon, Gayle. *Assuming a Body: Transgender and Rhetorics of Materiality.* New York: Columbia University Press, 2010.

———. "What's Critical about Critical Phenomenology?" *Puncta: Journal of Critical Phenomenology* 1, no. 1 (2018): 8–17. DOI: 10.31608/PJCP.v1i1.2.

Sedgwick, Eve Kosofsky. *Touching Feeling: Affect, Pedagogy, Performativity.* Durham: Duke University Press, 2003.

Singh, Julietta. *The Breaks: An Essay.* Minneapolis: Coffee House Press, 2021.

Still, Judith. *Derrida and Hospitality: Theory and Practice.* Edinburgh: Edinburgh University Press, 2010.

Terranova, Fabrizio, dir. *Donna Haraway: Story Telling for Earthly Survival.* Icarus Films, 2016.

Winnicott, D.W. "Further Thoughts on Babies as Persons." In *The Child, the Family, and the Outside World,* 75–82. London: Penguin Classics, 2021.

———. "Transitional Objects and Transitional Phenomena." In *Playing and Reality,* 1–34. London: Routledge, 2005.